GRAFFITI VERITE' 17 (GV17)
Special 1974 Commemorative Reissue Series

IMPRESSIONS

A Black Arts and Culture Magazine

Volume 1 Number 2
Original Publication: Spring 1975

Reissue for Educational & Historical Reference Use Only

Disclaimer:

All Promotional Advertisements, Store Addresses, Events, Telephone Numbers, Magazine Location, Product Sale Prices and Magazine Subscription information within the Original Publication issue are no longer, in most cases, in existence and/or applicable.

Please direct all inquires regarding the Special 1974 Commemorative Reissue of the GV17 IMPRESSIONS MAGAZINE (2012) to:

IMPRESSIONS MAGAZINE

c/o BRYAN WORLD PRODUCTIONS
P.O. Box 74033 Los Angeles, CA 90004 USA
website: www.graffitiverite.com
e-mail: bryworld@aol.com

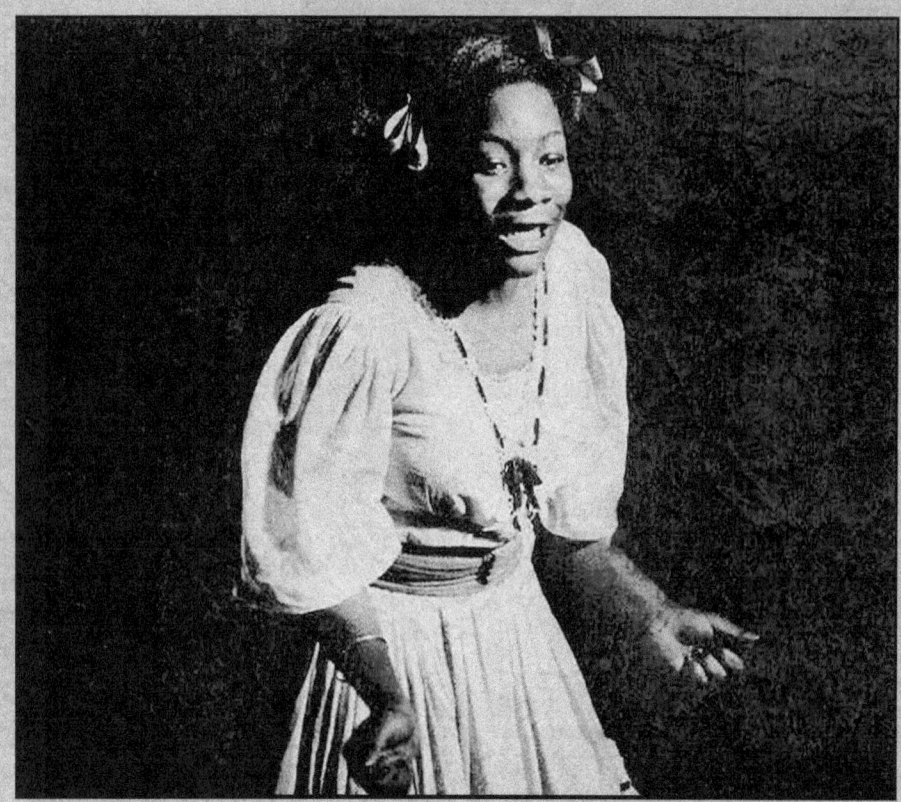

THE WIZ

1974, THE WIZ CO.

Majestic Theater
245 W. 44th Street
246-0730

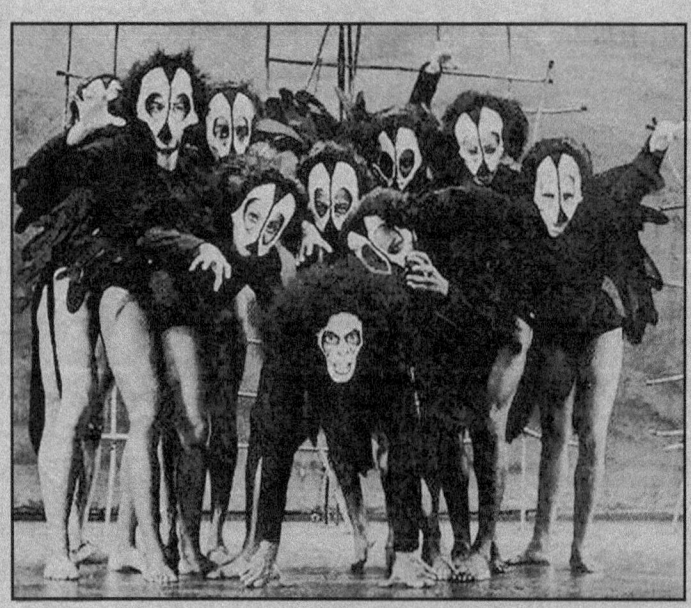

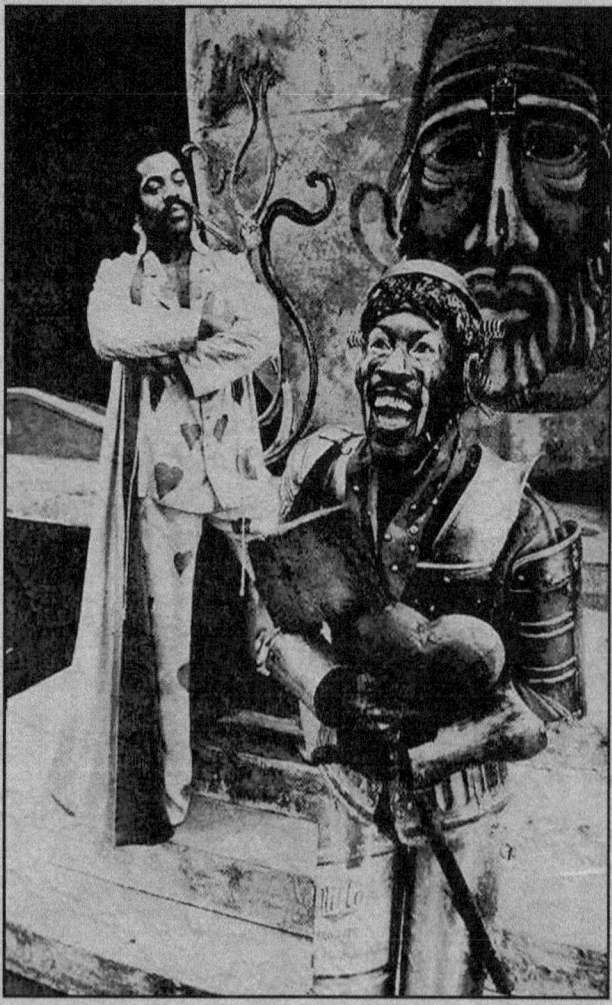

IMPRESSIONS

A Black Arts and Culture Magazine

VOL. I NO. 2   **SPRING '75**

CONTENTS

poetry

photography

Distribution Manager/Michael Barnes

Publisher
Robert Bryan

Art Director
Herb Henry

Literary Director
Baron James Ashanti

Editors
Calvin Wilson / Theater Reviews
Bob Wisdom / Jazz Notes
Brenda Bailey / Nutrition

FERN

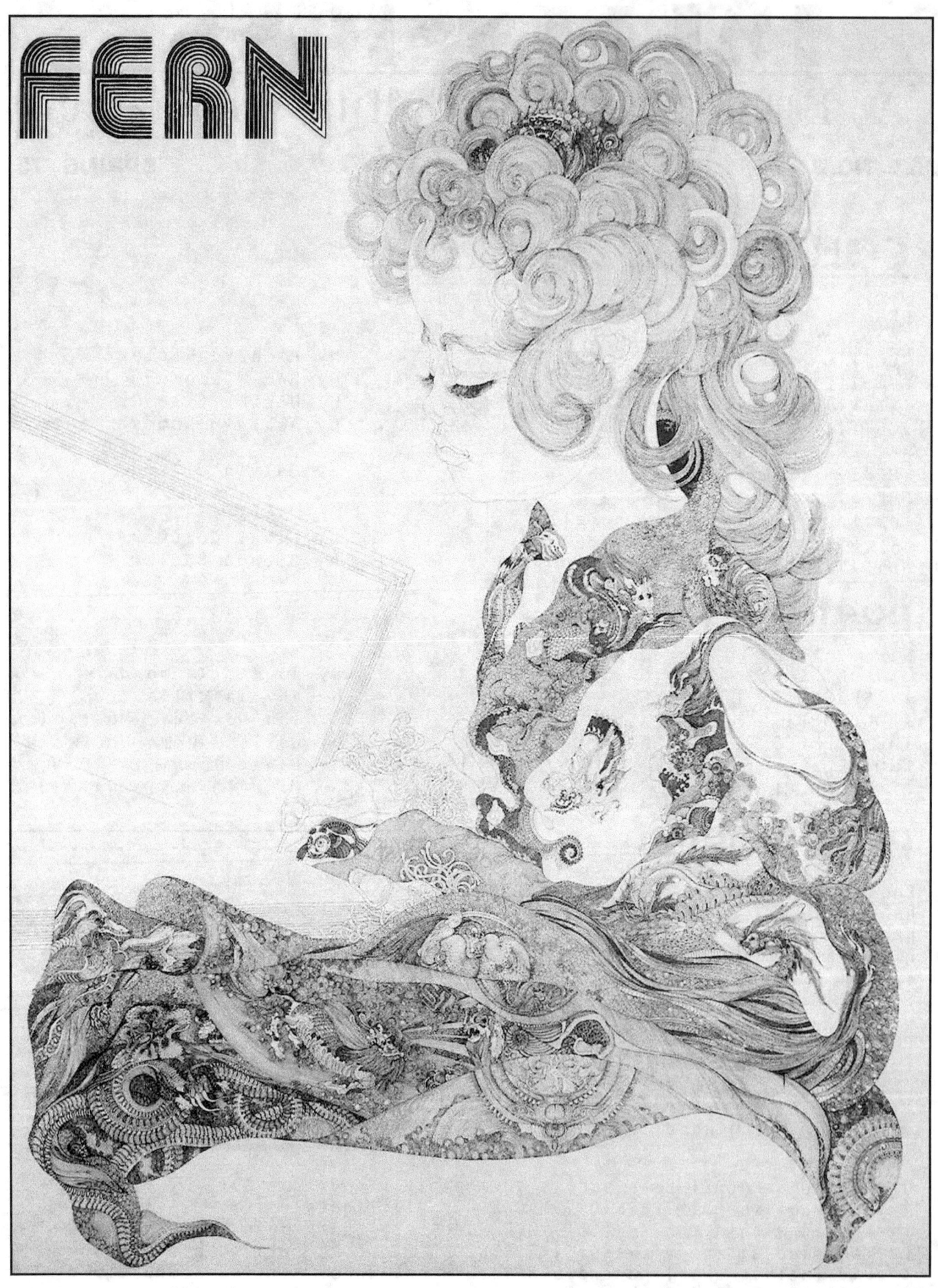

IAISHIA AND THE DAEMON COAT

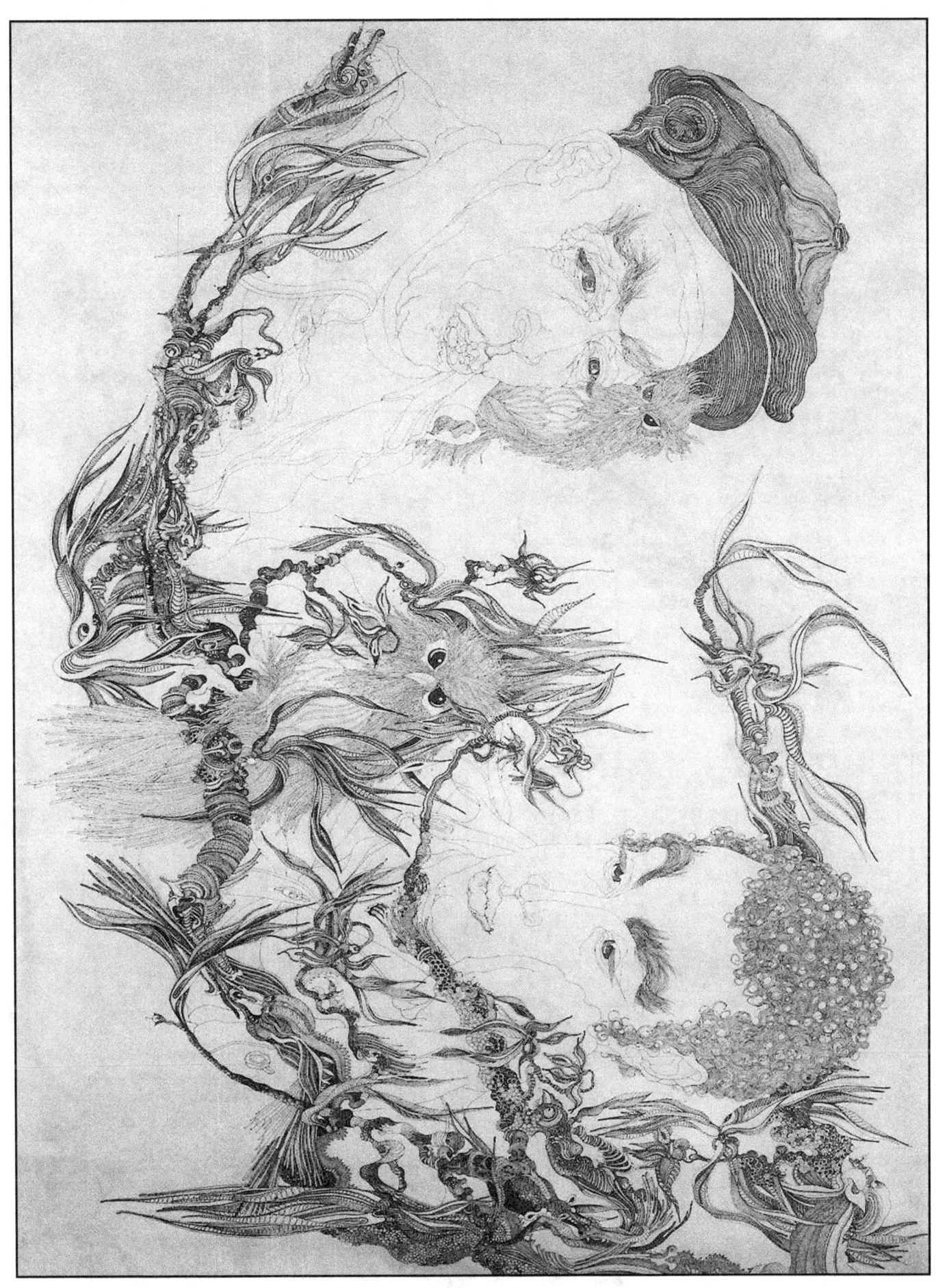

THE DAEMON BOUGH

Summary

My Song:
    A toast in bitter mirth-
    A strained and mocking jest
    Bubbling in clouded wine.

My Dream:
    A flame in dreariness-
    A dimly glowing lamp
    Hung in a throbbing dark.

My Self:
    A puff of crumbling earth-
    A cloud of saffron dust
    Caught in a purple wind.

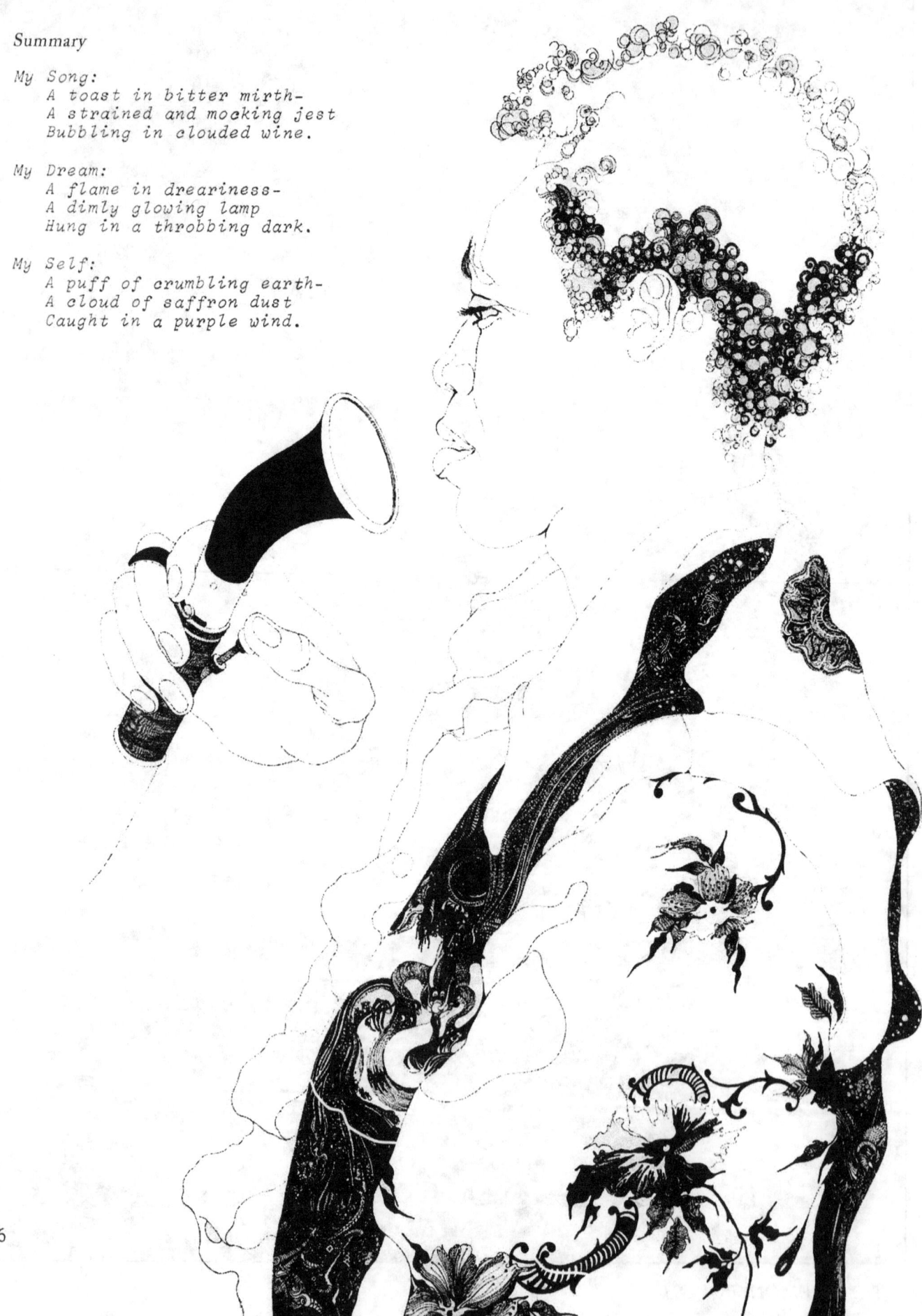

RICHARD WESLEY

POSITION PAPER ON BLACK THEATRE

As Black Theatre artists it is incumbent upon us to practice that which we were preaching in the 60's and effectively move to establish and maintain control over that body of work which we call Black Theatre Criticism. For, in these days of the 1970's, we are witnessing renewed attacks upon the integrity and legitimacy of Black Theatre presentations. We must do this by making Black Theatre a legitimate concern of the Black community at large, and not just the same Blacks who have supported Black Theatre all along. It is my contention that a large part of this burden must fall not only upon the artists themselves but also among those who have power within the world of Black-controlled media and magazines. We must begin to understand that it is patently unfair of nationally distributed Black-owned or oriented publications to talk primarily about movie and recording stars and deal only partially with Black Theatre. Is it not as equally important for the national Black community to know about BLACK PICTURE SHOW opening in New York as it is for us to know about Michael Jackson's acne problem? Is it not as equally important for the national Black community to know that THE WIZ is the best musical on Broadway as it is for us to know that Pam Grier dates Freddie Prinze off and on? Why is it that no Black publication ef-

fectively deals with theatre other than to mention a play or two here and there? There are more than 100 Black Theatres operating within the continental United States, presenting full seasons of plays and yet no one even knows of them. This is a terrible situation which must be corrected immediately. We must be publicized. The Audelco Awards in New York should be just as important to Blacks nationally as the Tony Awards are to the white folks. The NAACP Image Awards must be treated with the same respect in Black publications as the Oscars are treated in white publicatons. But this is just a beginning. Once we have made our theatre important, we must move to protect it at all costs.

For instance, the Village Voice recently ran a review of BLACK PICTURE SHOW by one of its critics who promptly dismissed it in a twelve-sentence review. He said, in effect, that he was wasting his time even bothering to write the review, and that white people would be wasting their time in going to see it. He found the play incoherent and inaccessible, his exact words. A lot of Blacks are into the Village Voice and once they read that article they might have decided not to see PICTURE SHOW while it was running. And, needless to say, a lot of whites who might have otherwise gone to see PICTURE SHOW were kept away by a supposedly "hip" white boy writing in a supposedly "hip, left, liberal, funky, far out and with it" newsweekly. Earlier, Rex Reed wrote a jive review in the Daily News in which he spewed forth his anger that Bloods had the audacity to do Wizard of Oz without resurrecting memories of Judy Garland and Bert Lahr. And what about SIZWE BANZI IS DEAD? It is obvious that this play was developed from the minds of the two great Xhosa actors we see onstage. It is a gut reaction that I felt as a Black man. But, all of the critics praised Afrikaner Athol Fugard for his amazing "insight" in writing this play. At best, he may have only devised a structure, but the content belongs to Kani and Ntshona and the experiences of their people.

The above-mentioned problems exist because we Blacks have not moved in affirmative enough directions to counteract the negative and uninformed things white critics say about our work.

A magazine like JET must feature a section in its entertainment department for reviews of plays that open on or off-Broadway. A program like SOUL TRAIN would do Black Theatre a great service if they would invite the cast of a touring Black play onto the show just so that the Black nation can SEE them and thence become aware of them. We should know as much about Carole Cole and Stephanie Mills nationally as we do about Carol Speed and Gloria Hendry. We should know, as a people, that there are more

directors, producers and actors working around the country on a steady basis in Black Theatre than there are in Black films, which are mostly white films, anyway. The Black media must take responsibility for getting this kind of information out to the Black public. Space must be given to Black critics so that they can gain access to the public mind. Not just on white newspapers where virtually none exist, but in Black publications, which thousands of Blacks read daily. Any Black magazine that specializes in entertainment should have a competent Black critic to cover theatre. Our magazines and newspapers must accept the reality that there is such a thing as Black theatre and stop trying to convince people that if it were not for Pam Grier we would have no Black actresses and that if it were not for Berry Gordy, there would be no Blacks in a position to call themselves "producers."

But once we have succeeded in making the Black Theatre and, by extension, the Black Critic important to the Black nation, we have to decide once and for all the answer to a major question that has been bandied about by Black artists since the mid-1960's when contemporary Black Theatre was in fruition. That question, simply put, is: Must the Black critic automatically give a favorable review to a show because it is Black, or must he apply standards of excellence to the work and demand that, in the name of the community, that work be up to par? The answer may seem obvious until one remembers that Black critics

continued on pg. 53

PROFILE:

Lonnie Liston Smith

BY BOB WISDOM

The music industry makes it's "Stars." Of course there have been the artist who were dominant, particularly in Jazz, who the string pullers allow to stand-as if these musicians needed their sanctions. But then there are the one's who hold up the industry by their consistency and their belief in their music. They may not particularly have "The Sound" that is currently leading the top 40's chart but what they do have is the seed from which that sound grows.

To further categorize a Jazz musician is a drag, but for perspectice sake-LONNIE LISTON SMITH is from that latter group. Lonnie's consistently beautiful sound is not only exotic in texture but extremely lyrical. His preence is definitely felt whenever he is on a set for his music is not merely supportive but is the type of music that is built around. On this basis and out of his own development comes the COSMIC ECHOES.

Lonnie has not arrived at this point without paying his dues. Coming out of Baltimore, his father was a member of the Harmonizing Four, a Spiritual Group. Lonnie played in the Morgan State Band and singing in the choir. He started playing sets in and around Baltimore before a desire to play with Max Roach pulled him to New York. He never recorded with Max Roach and Abby Lincoln but he did go on to play with Betty Carter, Al Hibbler and then his first recording session with Roland Kirk.

Lonnie is commonly identified with the "Pharoah Sanders Group." This concept is very interesting because this group was supposed to be

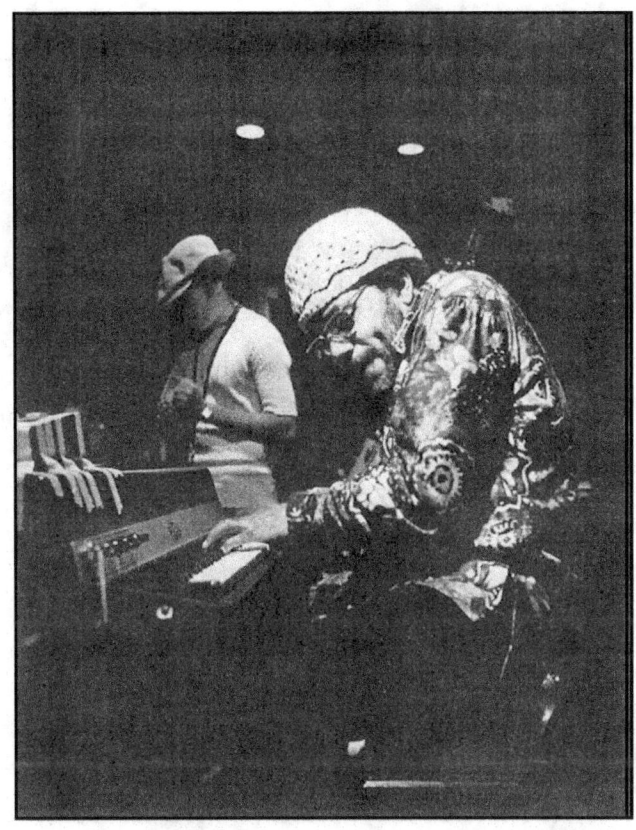

Photo by Bob Ellison

more of a collective rather than a one-man band. As the story goes, Lonnie and Pharoah kept bumping into each other as Lonnie was catching Pharoah's matinee sets at New York's old Slugs. As time went on each appreciated what the other was trying to do and finally looked to form along with Leon Thomas one of the most important new music groups of the late 60's and early 70's. But the growth of each member was going in different directions and through various differences the group disbanded, but not without making it's mark.

Lonnie then moved with Gato Barbieri whose group was not so free moving and didn't leave much

9

space for soloing. This occurred because "Gato,has a more definite idea of what he wants." Although Lonnie was limited in a stylistic sense Lonnie was provided with an understanding of Gato's "Third World Concept."

These groups and various business "expereences," specifically his not being credited on the Pharoah Sanders Karma album led to Lonnie's forming the COSMIC ECHOES. This group pulled together some of the finest new talent on the music scene. Mtume on percussion, David Lee on Drums, Cecil McBee on bass and George Baron on Tenor. The group works well primarily-as an observer aptly noted "No one seems to be playing for himself but to the others in the group..." The validity of this observation is confirmed in Lonnie's contention that "...when I play I hear a lot of instruments..."

Growth is the key to sustenance. What Lonnie Liston Smith has done is taken his personal growth and woven it into his music. The eastern philosophies that he studies manifest themselves in the melodious quality in his compositions. There is notthing bitter about Lonnie Liston Smith, there are no pretensions, no gimmicks. The musicians he has worked with have all been dedicated to their music, and as a result the music on his two albums *Astral Traveling and Cosmic Funk* both on Flying Dutchman is consistently progressive and inventive.

With three albums of his own on the Flying Dutchman label, Lonnie's growth can be concretely traced. The albums, *Astral Traveling, Cosmic Funk* and his latest *Expansions* all serve as testimony to Lonnie Liston Smith's growth and impact on the music world.

SUBSCRIBE TODAY! see p.3

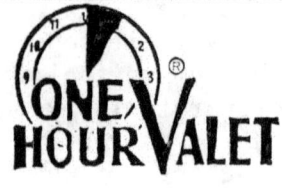
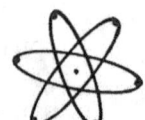

Wind Goddess:
Sound of Sculpture

(For *Doris Mayes* (Mezzo-Soprano), after March 17 (1970)
      recital, Conservatory, Oberlin College)

In *Beulahland!*
You highlystand.

Raped wind-hordes
Walled & wailing against unforgotten gates
At your back.

Meticulously led,
These rough airs
Come sculpted,
Amplified,
Like African arrows,
From the silkly camouflaged turbulence
& beauty of your middlecountry.

Here is no sun-forsaken soul,
As that ancient light leaps
& smiles its rainbow of sounds
From your -
Now choiric/ancestral
Then epic/soulo -
Voice,
Vexing cured chant, and...
"*Everytime* I feel the spirit...."

From *Sentry of the Four Golden Pillars*

In Search of Destiny

(for Mijack)

our vision is to
answer
the soul's inquiry:
is there security in
uncertainty?
a place between
be/tween?

we harbor gutted
fears
that dictate
love can be a
shelter
or like
dust
settled for a
rest

but time is a
current
draggin dreams through
oppressive memories
    leadin us
to share private
realisms:
as nomads
we carry only
faith in love,

so we chase dreams
at night
between decisions
that ride on the
wind.....

RHONDA MILLS lives in New York City. She attended Long Island University. She is published in CONFRONTATION, and BLACK WORLD (Long Island). She was a member of the Chuck Davis Dance Company and has a forthcoming volume of poems titled Dark Heat When the Sun Go Down.

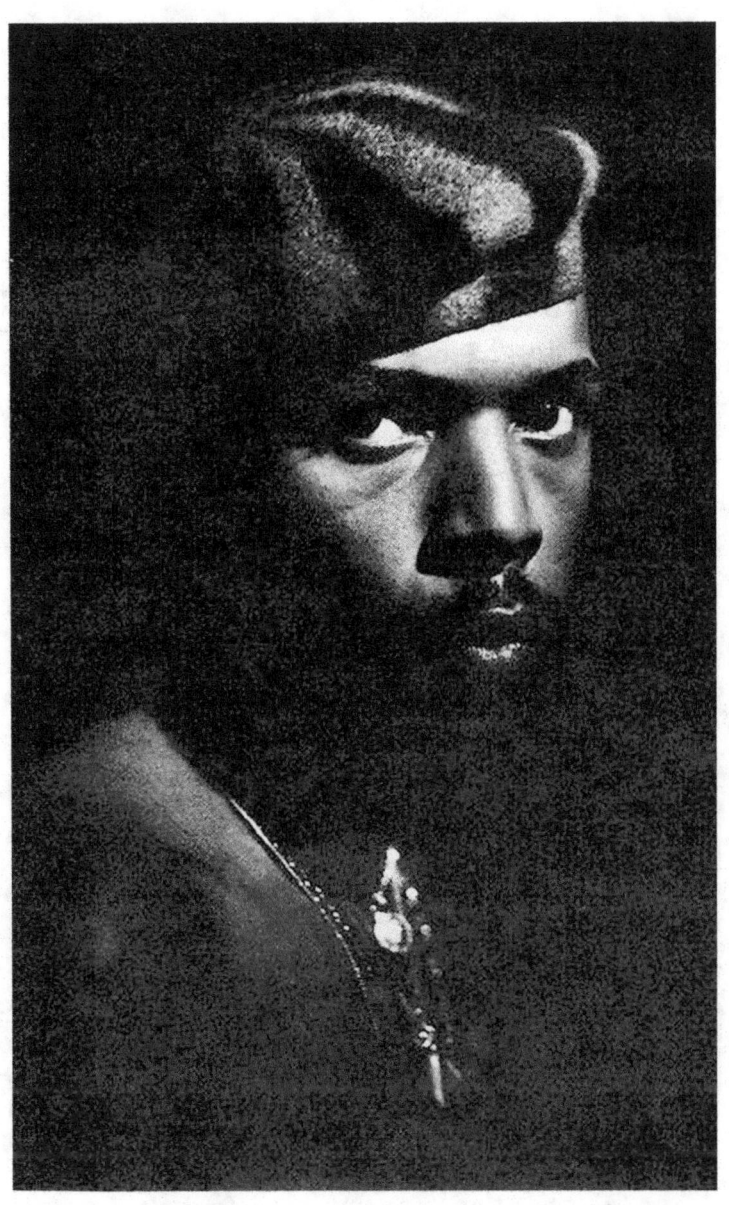

Bob Bryan

(Subject: Cleveland Keeler)

INTERVIEW WITH:

BILL GUNN

Writer, Director of THE BLACK PICTURE SHOW & GANJA & HESS

Written by R. Bryan

Interview by Hector Lino, Jr.

Hector: When you're sitting down and writing, do you approach the paper first with an idea or do you sit down and then write anything that comes out, sort of like automatic writing until something happens?

Bill: I sit down with a thing and then I do it. The idea unfolds itself and creates itself as I do it. Whenever I sit down with the whole thing it comes out stiff, I like it to create itself right there-let the characters come to life. I used to sit down with an outline, with a beginning, middle and end and I swear I have yet to follow that outline. One outline I started so many times it finally turned out to be 5 different pieces of work for me.

Hector: Bill, what's your background; where did you grow up?

Bill: I guess you might call it a middle class black family. The schools I went to very early were always integrated, but they always treated you as if you weren't there. So, they threw me out of school in my 2nd year of H.S. They said, I wasn't listening. That's the reason they gave, that I wasn't paying attention.

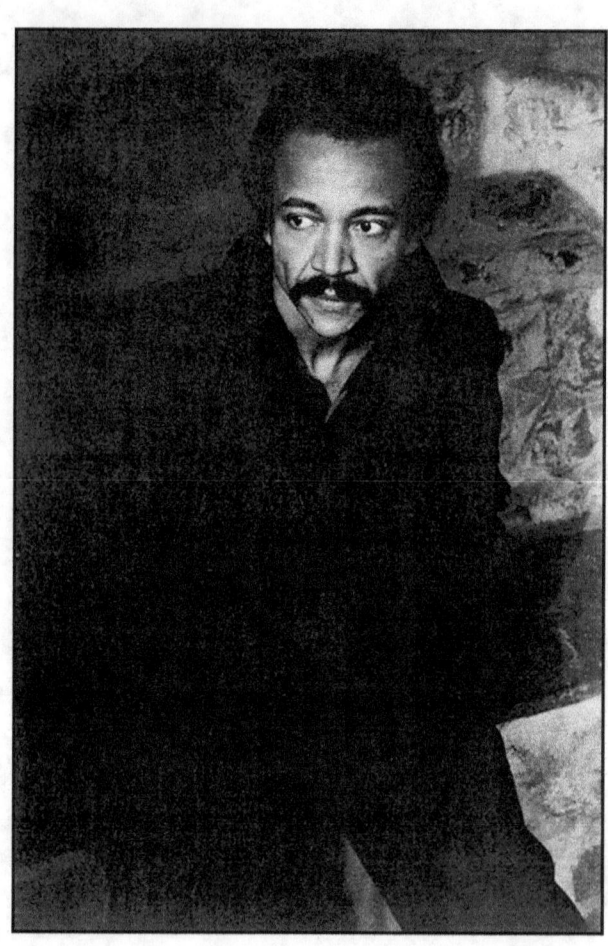

Hector: Were you?

Bill: No, they weren't paying attention to me. I spotted that. I learned what I had to; I learned to read and write and how to add, subtract and I left there and went into my own thing. I started to read- I read quite a bit.

Hector What were some of the things that you were reading?

14

Bill: Well, you know in middle class families back then there isn't an enormous amount of books around. They don't deal with that, they sort of push that education thing on you, but once you drop out of that they're not really interested in the fact that you're creative. So I was a victim of that, but my parents are really sensitive people. They would have much preferred if I had gone off and been a doctor.

Hector: Of the novels that you read, who were some of the people that you dug?

Bill: I read Oscar Wilde very early; my father came home with a complete set of Horatio Alger books-I read every one of them. I read some Negro Digest, that were around. They came to the house.

Hector: Did you get anything out of that?

Bill: Well yes, my father didn't like it so he stopped them from coming. He thought it was doing things to my head. I like biographies.

Hector: Why do people's lives have a particular interest to you?

Bill: I liked Alexander the Great. He really got me.

Hector: Why?

Bill: Because not only did they say that it was real, but it was fantastical too. I wasn't really interested in Madame Curry or George Washington Carver. It was too real, too basic. I don't know, it just attracted me. History is interesting; I like history.

Hector: When did you become interested in making movies?

Bill: Really...really? As I look back now, I think I got started when I was around six, 'cause I remember taking a Brownie Camera and setting it up for some reason or another. I'd set things up with light coming through the window: glass, apple or drape a piece a piece of material with the light on and I'd try to see it thru the camera. But for some reason I wasn't interested in still photography. I had no interest in that whatsoever. But then I built a stage and I started moving things around but I had to see them close up. You could stand back and see it as a play but I wanted to see their expressions on their faces. So the only way I could deal with that was to relive it constantly. I was the only child. The movies were 10¢ and it was nice, I was very quiet and so I went to the movies and I didn't get into any trouble so my parents said "cool". It was like a baby-sitter. So I was seeing everything. The first film that really took me off was Sir Lawrence Olivier and Vivian Leah in (unclear). Here it was coming at me at a really creative level, it was a romance. History is really a romance.

Hector: Did you ever see film as a weapon to influence people?

Bill: I think it's really incredible. I never saw it as a weapon when I was attracted to it. I saw it as a very creative thing where I could create my own world. I could create my own people and not just writing them down but actually take physical bodies and create places and situations and set people down and create an entire world. Very aware even as a little child that I was sitting in the mist of somebody elses world looking at a movie. Not their reality, but their world (entire), everything. If a couple was walking down the street in a movie and there was a building behind them or a traffic jam or whatever, it was he that created that. He made me see what he wanted me to see. Everything that existed up there on the screen, existed in his world. It was incredible, you go and watch an early Cagney film or a George Raff film about prison and there's a prison riot And there isn't one "F-ck" in the entire dialogue. There's someone controlling that. Presenting that prison riot to you thru their own reality. So it isn't a real riot, it becomes a figment of someones imagination.

Hector: Is the aspect of control the fascinating thing?

Bill: It was control, but not just controlling it, or else I would be a Hitler. But it's that I could put the world exactly where I thought it should be. Which was in a very beautiful place. I mean that's where my head was as a child. I was a very strange child. Everything had to be very beautiful. only my sense of beauty. The fantastical things really fascinated me the most.

Hector: Such as...?

Bill: Ah...I got very hung up on Dorothy Lamore-John Hall movies because everything was unreal. The grass was obviously paper grass, and the stream

was not real and off in the distance were paste board hills; it was so tacky and the lights-you could see it. That was really incredible. Look at these people, they're giving us a picturebook and everybody in the theater is really taking off on it. You know...And that fascinated me more. I always knew that in those days that everything was unreal. I always knew that you could move into the street, off the set.

Hector: So you weren't trapped like Bigger Thomas (ED. NOTE: SEE RICHARD WRIGHT'S NATIVE SON) You always knew that you could change your reality if you wanted to...

Bill: Yes. I was fascinated with what they were doing. It was always THEY. I was very aware that there wasn't any black faces up there, and the few black faces that were up there: butlers, maids and things- they never bothered me, cause I never identified with them.

Hector: Where were THEY in terms OF YOUR REALITY?

Bill: They were pasteboard figures. I never connected them. Some older people would look and be a little insulted. This was terrible but then I would think why would they think that this had anything to do with them.

Hector: What's your family relationship like?

Bill: Very good. We're very close.

Hector: Who influenced you the most?

Bill: Probably my mother,

continued on pg. 45

RENNIE GEORGE

RENNIE GEORGE is a free-lance photographer from the Bronx, N.Y. C. Rennie's a graduate of The High School of Art & Design, WNET film workshop, and is now attending Fordham University. His work has been published in various publications, including the BLACK PHOTOGRAPHERS ANNUAL. The following portfolio was taken in various countries of West Africa.

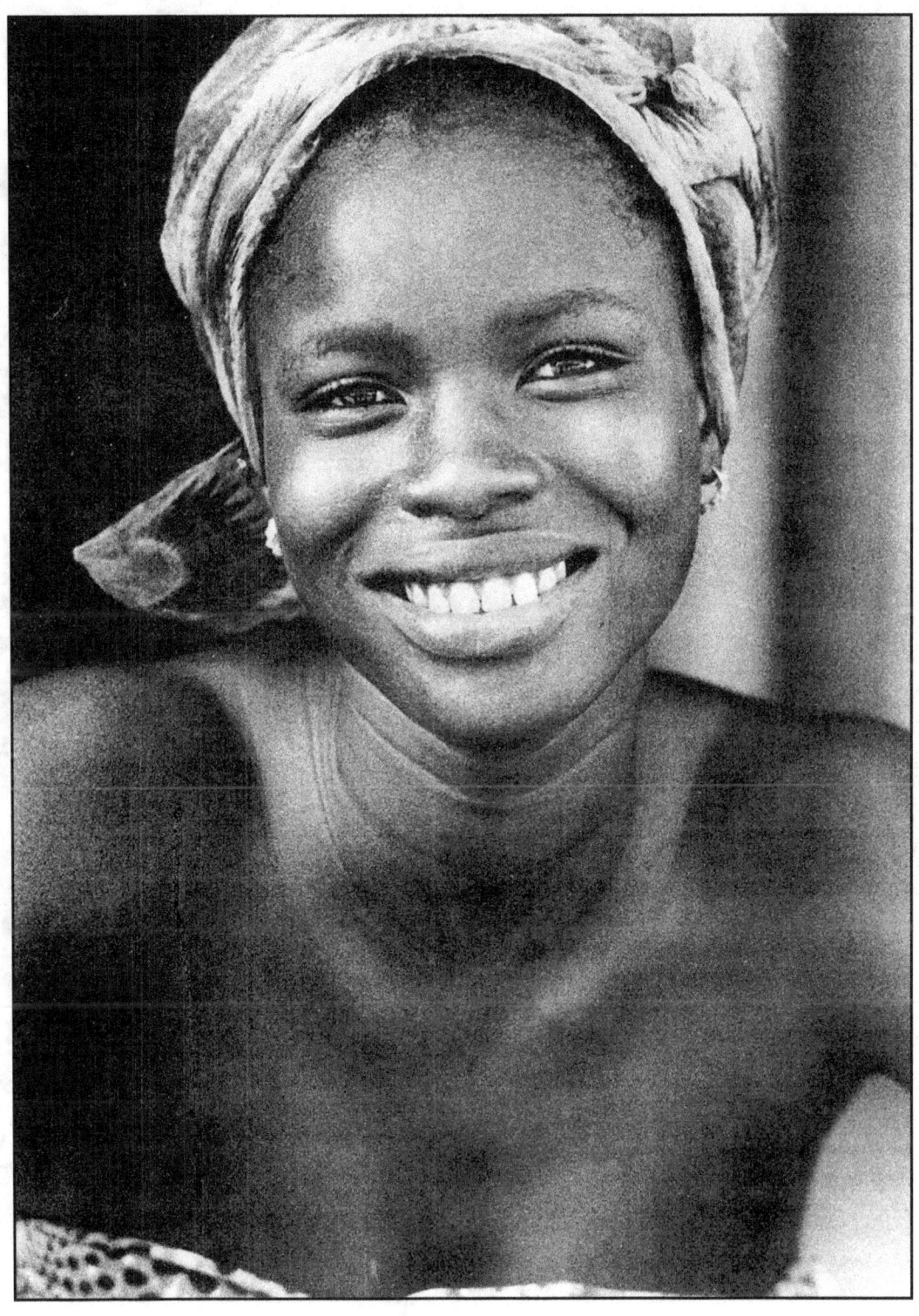

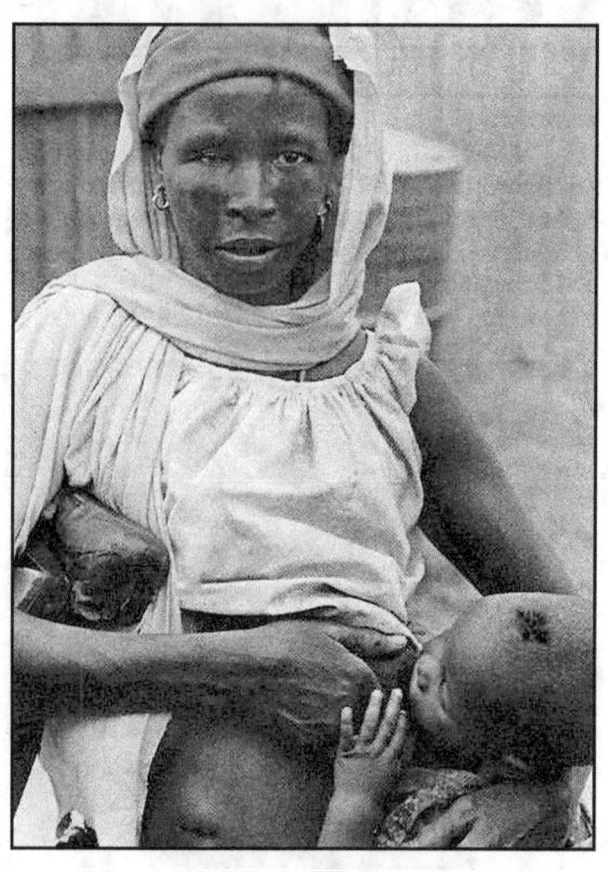

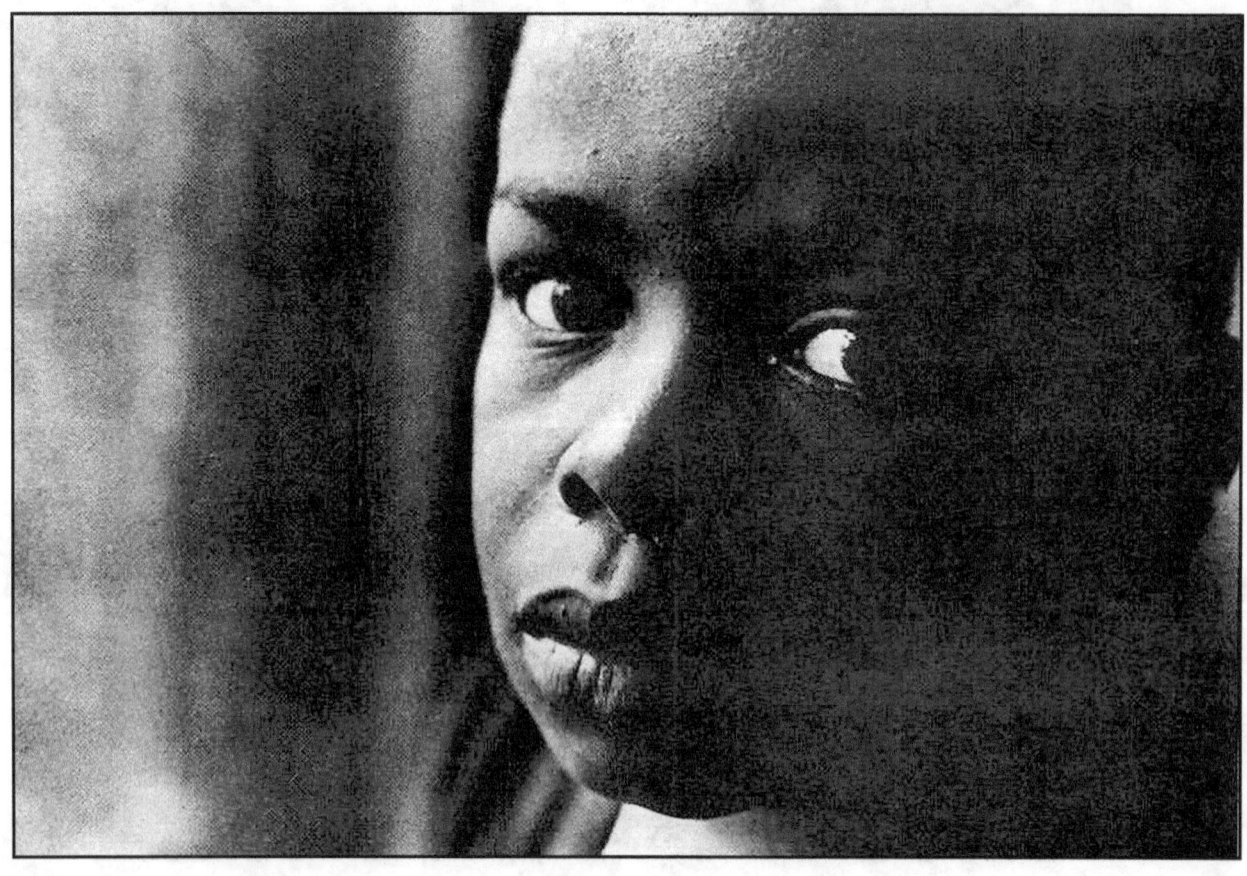

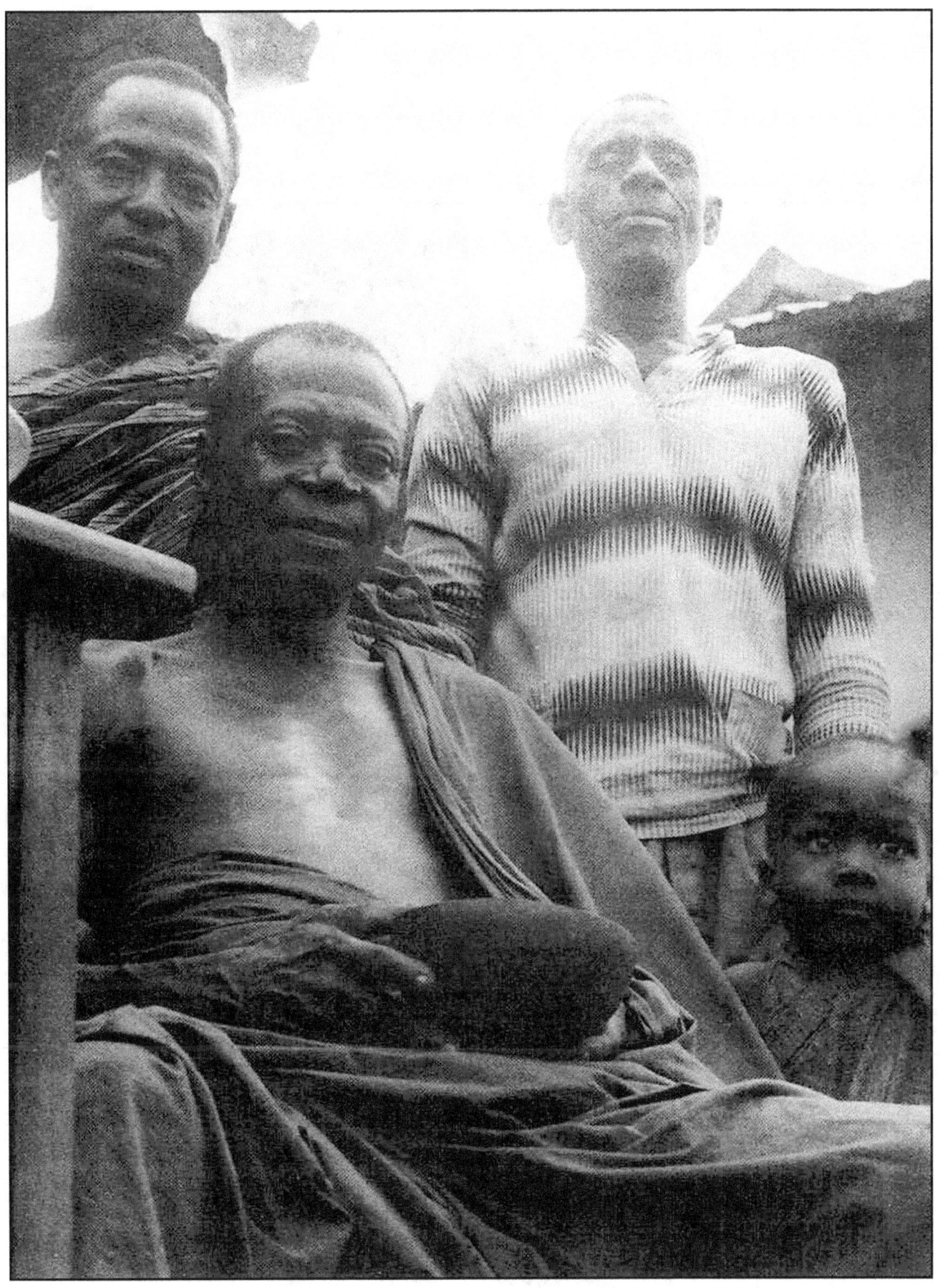

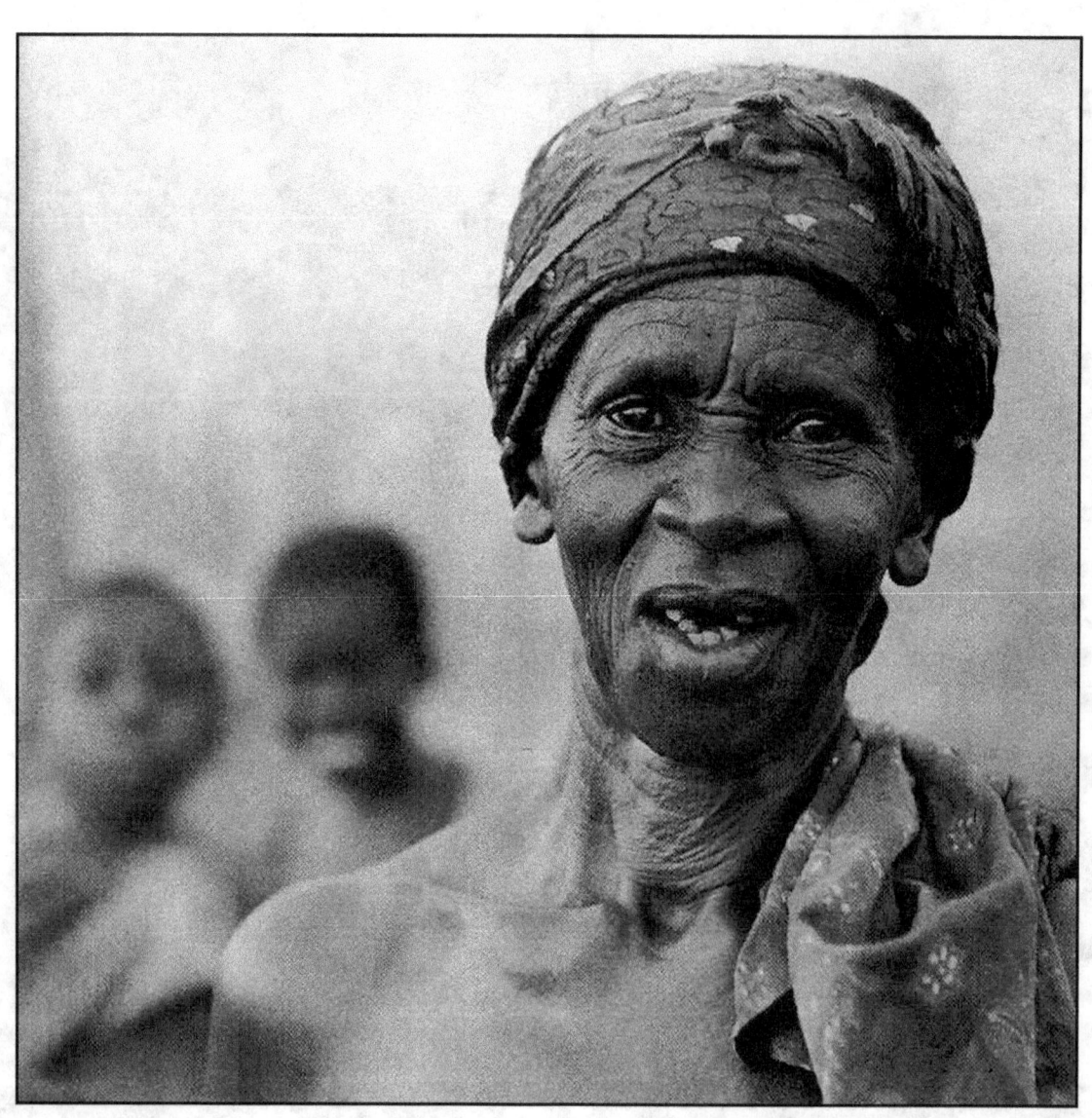

Askia Muhammad Toure's Position Paper

Afro-Amerikan Writer's Conference

Brother Toures' position paper was given at the auspicious occasion of the Afro-Amerikan Writers' conference, held at D.C. Howard University in December of last year ('74). Brother Toure read his paper during a poetry panel which included Kalamu Ya Salaam, Mari Evans, Haki Mahadbuti and Quincy Troupe. On the last day of the conference a small workable nucleus of about 70 writers got down and did the do. The unanimous call that came from the floor was for the formation of a National Black Writers' organization. This was not a regional call but a national call. The national steering committee which was elected consists of such people as: Toni Cade Bambara, John Oliver Killens, Piri Thomas, Lorenzo Thomas, Marvin X, Baron James Ashanti, Haki Mahadbuti, Askia M. Toure,etc (all the names for the steering committe are not given here because they are not available.) The first meeting for the steering committee will be in March at Howard University. See y'all there.

lit. ed. note

P.S. Interruptions in the delivery of the position paper are given in full here because they set the atmoshere for the conference and also for the poetry panel discussion which Bro. Toure participated in.

I'm going to be reading from my paper, the introduction of my paper, "Towards the Consolidation of an Afro-American National Liberation." One of the things that I want to call to your attention which has, frankly irritated me, is I keep getting echoes of a funny kind of line that's been threading its way through this conference about the 60's being nothing but rap, being jive. Yet we have mountains of dead. We've lost two great leaders; we lost young heros like Ralph Featherstone and George Jackson and Ruby Dora Smith Robertson, etc. We have lost from the masses of our people in Newark, Detroit and Los Angeles, and people are going to run to us and say it was jive. You tell that to our people out in the street- the masses of our people who suffered and who put their courage on the line-that the 60's was jive; those people who got eaten by those dogs down in Birmingham and got the doggone fire hoses put on them, that the 60's was jive. Anytime this power structure feels threatened enough to wipe out your major leaders, that movement is not jive (applause). So, with that I'm going to get into my introduction (laughter).

In this brief introduction, I will attempt to sketch an overview of meaning and impact of the Black Arts, Black Aesthetic movement and its revolutionary initiation of a qualitative change in the directions and goals of African Culture in America.

The Black Arts Movement, which began in the mid-sixties, was built upon the foundation of three revolutionary nationalist journals, created by young black nationalist artist-activists. These original journals were Soul Book, 1964; Black Dialogue,

1965; and The Journal of Black Poetry, 1966. The authors of the journals, all of which contained national rather than regional editorial boards, consciously chose their roles as initiators of a far-reaching cultural revolution in black literature. The term artist-activist is a key to the understanding of this cultural revolution and its subsequent history. The authors, while being creative artists, were also political activists participating in the Black Liberation Struggle which surfaced as the Black Power Movement in the late 60's. The authors were members of a younger generation which emerged into adulthood at a period of almost cataclysmic change in world events. This was the anti-colonial era of the late 1950's and early 1960's which contained the interrelated phenoma of the First Bandung Conference in Bandung, Indonesia, of former colonial peoples, the rise of Dr. Nkrumah's Ghana via the re-emergence of African peoples, and the Cuban, Algerian and Zanzibar revolutions. This was also a period of peak influence of such thinkers and international personalities as Dr.Nkrumah, Padmore, Franz Fanon, Patrice Lumumba, Bro. Malcolm X and Robert F. Williams upon the modern mass movement of Blacks in America which began in and interrelated with this period.

In this retrospect, it is almost redundant to state that these events and personalities created a qualitative change in the consciousness and world view of this generation, forever separating it from the values, attitudes and goals of its predecessors. This is worth noting when confronted with cliche analysis between the Black Arts Movement and the Harlem Renaissance. The Harlem Renaissance, and all respect to our great elders, as projected by, I would say, its leading theoretician, Dr. Alain Locke, seemed to be an assimilationist movement, lead by artists and critics, backed by white patrons geared towards partnership between blacks and whites in building an "American" national culture. The Black Arts, Black Aesthetics Movement, in the words of noted critic, Addison Gayle, was "pushed into actuality by the Black Power Movement of the 60's to serve as the cultural arm of the Black Nationalist Movement." We will explore this phenomenon later. The Black Arts Movement swept across America like Garvey's famous whirlwind, creating a new radical consciousness which manifested itself in such forms as the Black Student Movement, the Black Studies Movement, the Black Theater Movement and, of course, the new Black writing. Needless to say, authors of the revolutionary journals were active participants and, in some cases, initiators of these movements and programs.

Towards the end of the sixties, when it became apparent that Black America was indeed in the throes of a cultural revolution, new elements entered the fray. Representing the ever-conscious cultural elements of the Black bourgeoisie, these forces began to reshape and redefine the aims of the Black Arts Movement. Lacking the experience of having initiated the movement, but motivated by a crusading zeal to "make a contribution," they made major mistakes both in historical analysis and related strategy. It is to this element that we owe the erroneous comparison of Black Arts to the Harlem Renaissance and, more dangerously, the spread of corroding western values within the literary movement. Younger writers, lacking the experience and social vision, were inflated to the rank of superstar and thrust into leadership roles which they were unequipped to play. The rise of the superstars, promoted by popular bourgeois magazines in the east and the west, divided the literary movement, which was based on African collective values, by introducing the western phenomena of indiviualism and competition (applause). See Dingane/Goncalves critiques on Haki Mahdabuti's "Dynamite Voices" in the West Indian Edition of The Journal of Black Poetry.

In spite of the many setbacks and the current madness (laughter), including betrayal by current opportunists and attacks by Hollywood and mass media, our cultural revolution continues to flourish. While some of the original journals were casualties to the late 60's, others continue to publish, joined by scores of new regional journals across the country. Another encouraging development is the growing number of guerilla presses that have surfaced since the early seventies. They are joined by the expansion of workshops and collectives developed by the newest strata of young writers. And, as a final stage in our evolution, we have been gifted with a growing body of well trained, perspective young critics who are intimate with the writers and their work. When these phenomena are examined and evaluated, one becomes aware of the rise of a national intelligentsia for Black America.

As encouraging as these latest developments seem, it would be utmost folly to rely solely on the spontaneity of the movement. We must consciously work to bring the cultural revolution to a new stage by creating a national congress to guide the movement of Black writers (applause). This body headed by a democratically elected, collective, leadership must serve to consolidate & guide the thinking of Black writers on the various questions of aesthetics and crafts and creative values. Equally important, one of its main tasks would be to develope strategies and tactics to improve the conditions for Black writers in America, coupled with the additional and important strategies that define the role of culture in our national struggle, in our national struggle (applause). Only when such a body has been freely created and is quietly pursuing the business of developing and expanding the realms of Black Literature can we say that we have

truly developed and consolidated an African National Literature in America. How about that? (Applause and words of approval and encouragement from audience) This is important because there's a whole lot of madness out here, out and out madness. We don't have to always agree, but I don't think anyone on this panel is an apologist for the oppression of Black people; I know that as a matter of fact. I've been holding information and part of this is my fault and maybe even Ed's (Spriggs). Maybe some of it's our fault; we din't say things ealier. I tried to say something in Black Dialogue when I was one of the editors, Winter/Spring 1967/67 Black Dialogue, in terms of the first, as far as I know, critiques of cult figures by one of their peers. For my outspokenness, I was reviled across this country and met with a climate of paranoia and hysteria because I had dared to criticize a black "genius," a "prophet" and a "father" of the Black Arts Movement.

With that introduction, I want to get into this. There was no father or prophet of the Black Arts Movement, and I can say it because I was there. The Black Arts Movement was a collective movement coming out of black people, and we had all kinds of sisters and brothers, critics and poets together, working with the masses of the people. This movement was not elitist at all because it was on the street with the masses of our people, not only on the east coast but in the midwest and on the west coast. This was not an elitist movement, and it was not a movement, I repeat, lead by any kind of "father" or reactionary cult figure (laughter & applause). (Question from audience: "Who are you talking about?") I'm talking about Amiri Baraka, and I wish he were man enough to be here. (Question from audience: Excuse me, was he invited here?) Yes. Haki said he invited him here. (Comment

continued on pg. 50

LIFELINES

THEATER REVIEWS

by Calvin Wilson

The Island is a naturalistic depiction of several days in the lives of two men imprisoned on Robben Island in South Africa. The crimes which they committed are never spelled out, but we are led to believe that the men have been brought there for political actions against the state. We know that this island is Robben Island in South Africa only because the devisers of the play have provided this information. In the same way, we assume that the two men have been sentenced to prison terms for acts of defiance against the institutional, legal racism of South Africa.

The two Black men who play the prisoners are also responsible for the creation of this play through their collaboration with a white South African playwright. Athol Fugard, who is also known for his plays The Blood Knot and Boesman and Lena, has acquired a reputation both as a fine dramatist and as a critic of his country's policy of apartheid. When he met actors John Kani and Winston Ntshona in 1962, the two men had finished high school and were working with a small Black theater group called The Serpent Players. They could not afford to go to college because they had already paid for high school and had no money to go further with their education. In South Africa, in accordance with the apartheid laws, primary and secondary school is free and compulsory for whites but not for non-whites.

Impressed with Kani and Ntshona, Fugard lent his theatrical expertise to the Serpent Players, guiding them through the works of such playwrights as Genet and Brecht. Finally, when he felt that the group was ready for work more relevant to the political climate of South Africa, Sizwe Banzi is Dead was brought into the repertoire. Like The Island, it was devised by Kani, Ntshona and Fugard.

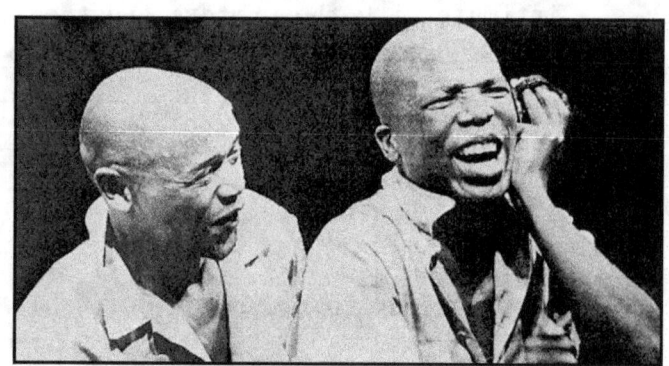

Under Fugard's direction, The Island conveys the tedium and oppression of prison life. At one point in the play, the two prisoners, talking in their cell, reflect upon the state of a fellow prisoner. Much older than the two characters on stage, this third man which they refer to has become a husk whose life revolves around the tasks he must perform in the prison workyard. In order to preserve their own identity, the two men decide to put on a performance of a scene from Antigone. They intend to use her moral predicament in the face of the state to express their own resistance to the politics of Robben Island and South Africa.

Because there are only two characters in the play, the focus upon them is intense. This is established in the first twenty minutes of the play. During this first scene, there is no dialogue; we watch the two actors as they mime the act of shoveling dirt into holes, after which they run around the set as if doing laps around a track. The relationship between the two prisoners is one of resistance of a system which seeks to dehumanize them just as it has dehumanized the fellow prisoner upon which they comment. They talk to themselves, wait for letters from home and rehearse Antigone. Since the role requires that one of them dress as a woman, there is some debate between them about the possible reaction from the other prisoners in seeing such a performance. This issue is put aside when they decide that the prisoners will know that true manhood has nothing to do with the way a person dresses.

So dependent have the two men become upon each other that a crisis occurs, when John (John Kani) is informed that his petition for a reduced sentence has been successful and he has only two more months to serve. John's fellow prisoner Winston (Winston Ntshona) is happy for his friend, but bitter because he realizes that he will probably never be freed. In anger and confusion, Winston tells John that he will forget the prison and the people he knew there as soon as he is released. John denies this while puzzling over whether the prison authorities are trying to trick him into doing his work less efficiently so that they can punish him.

Because the South African government does not accept "artist" as an employment category, Kani and Ntshona are officially acknowledged by that government as household employees of Fugard. Before opening its Broadway run, The Island and

Sizwe Banzi is Dead played to great success in London. The plays were presented earlier in South Africa itself, where Kani, Ntshona and other members of the Serpent Players must wait until they have finished performing their day jobs (Kani was a Ford employee, Ntshona a lab assistant) in order to get into their roles as actors. Since they cannot be paid for being actors, their day jobs are necessary for income.

In a less severe way, Fugard has also suffered persecution from the South African government. In 1968, the government refused to grant him a passport to visit England in order to help in the television production of one of his plays and in 1970 the government would not allow him to visit New York, where he planned to assist in the production of Boesman and Lena. Fugard has managed to escape government censorship of plays which would be at odds with the apartheid policies by staging them in private homes. These private homes must be owned by whites since the privacy of Blacks are not honored.

Fugard does not agree with the theater world's boycott against South Africa. Many playwrights refuse to become involved with South Africa out of a feeling of protest, but Fugard argues that such an attitude achieves nothing and only serves to keep new ideas out of the country. He believes that playwrights should have their works produced in South Africa on the condition that the plays be taken out to the African townships as well as the urban areas. A large majority of Blacks and a few whites in South Africa feel that any condemnation of racism is worth the price.

Although born in South Africa, Fugard spent most of his early youth as a seaman and journalist. It was not until 1958, when working as a clerk in Johannesburg, that Fugard witnessed the inhuman treatment of

continued on pg. 54

Blood Debt Series:
Lake Chad 1

Hunted down by thirst
Ambushed
And stripped by scurvy
Humiliated
by harmattan-hunger
he drank from
the quivering dehydrated hairy carcasses
the wind by Gog
Danced nil in a delightful coma
and the dead never buried the dead
On the ninth day the sea became
A Prehistoric sand throne
A she camel slept her death
beside a caked water hole
Uncle lost his donkey
the bishop lost his easter Cow
the fields were bald
All rain makers and prophets failed
and it was over for the Ancient Combatant
the earth opened its belly
to receive a Sullen love
O lake Chad in you
Our hunger remains breathlessly strong
Stomachs like Palm Kernels. Hard.
Is this the way you feed your Children Africa?
Weep? we stopped, the people too can't cry
Africa is it peacetime?

Now I ask a question.

The Ripples of the Apocalypse

A pogrom sweeter than orgasm
ascent upon a mount of hatchet and fire.
Came the war and denial with the finality
of spades on sod where love was buried.

Men of my birth, think of the ripples of Apocalypse,
you who spill your sperm on pebbles by your threshold,
and pursue mice while flames dance on the crowns of your huts;
for on that day the rivers, even the mighty ones,
will turn to stone, and trees will rush like warriors
across the wilds, and the ivory beads around
the necks of your maidens will turn to cobras.

> *The sin of my people*
> *upon my people*
> *cannot be cleansed*
> *by the blue waters of Oguta.*

There was a time
before the death of the Moon
when apes lived in the forest,
a time when all the malignant things
that crawl through grass and brushes
passed indifferent to our cause.
But now all the demons have returned with hatchets
and spades, and lizards sharpen their teeth
on our senews.

> *The sin of my people*
> *against my people*
> *will not be cleansed*
> *by the fountain on Ibuzu.*

Heaven and Earth listen to our cry.
Songs of wind and leaves...
mud-smudged twigs on mounds.
Songs of sword and limbs
mould the soil for harvest.
The dead have buried us in their embrace.
Roots of the sun-flower fart in the air.
Shoots below caress the worms that in search of melody
blow in vain the flutes of our bones.

The ripples of the Apocalypse
peep through the cracks among our clouds,
waiting for the voice to roll the drums
to the gulf, and the flames of revelation dance red
among the edges of the Sky.

Ossie Onuora Enekwe
New York
1973

Sebastian Clarke

EXTRACT FROM HIS NEW NOVEL   Chapter 23

The room filled with black faces and Nini's tall and slender legs was a sight that the eyes fastened to. Her voice high and so soft it was a baby's world. The clean shavened face man tall and dark called Osei was touching Alex's legs and whispered to him of her beauty. Jabu named Alex a word familiar to her ears now seen. Everything was a longing in their eyes and soft flesh curled across legs was the vision of projected thirst and lust in their skins. There was nothing much to say and Jabu in his usual self laughed hysterically and slapped the outstretched palms of the small-bodied moustached man, Abdullah who grinned and his laugh was a voice sucking air. Nini surveyed the room which in bright colours and prints against walls was not her mind's idea of home but it filled her with feeling. Abdullah's wife called Nini and she was in the kitchen preparing food for the men. Everything was placed and women were subjected to the wishes and fulfillment of men who filled with the blessings of a reincarnating African history used elements in distortion that raised themselves. Nini filled with the meaning and a duty for her life was devotion and care in the men's eyes. And with her passing of the food a flood of consciousness through blood light with memory in growing to life now lived. The sun washed with dreaming eyes was a child living in a world guided to years of projected growth. And time had ceased. In the sudden seizure of the brain she was before the laughing face of her father returned from the length of a journey and so filled with joy was beyond the moving clouds. Relived she was before their faces a girl of pleasing ways.

Alex refused the food and ready for departure he said goodbye. Nini quickly moving from the room was behind the body on the stairs. "Are you leaving so soon?" "Yes, there are other things that I have to do." "Oh well, I suppose we'll be seeing each other since I'll be visiting here, making my contribution as it were." "I'll see. Well , take care." "Goodbye."

That night so late it was beyond the time of trains. Jabu had taken Osei in his car and there was nowhere she could go. Abdullah so willing she was given a room to sleep. Here in this dark room with the change so quick and feeling her body with a life she did not live and senses she could not feel washed and cleansed her brain. Everything so changed and these men so filled with intelligence it was a delight to be here. So much laughter and so much strength. And with the image and dream of her baby's safety sucking the last waves of consciousness before sleep the door opened. Abdullah stood naked at the door, his body tight with longing and desire. Who is it? The wind touched the window and it was a dead bird's fall in sunlight of the past. Who is it? The wind sighed and swept against the window, the curtain rose and parted. It is me. He was in the bed, his hand so hot it was steel against her flesh. What are you doing? His hands upon her thighs and crawling along her fleshy mass. What about yr wife? Don't you care? He climbed onto her and she crossed her legs. His mouth was fire on her breasts and her arms on his shoulder pressing him away. His prick in his fingers so hard it was lead searching for her cunt. No! Please don't! He placed both his arms between her legs and so quickly parted he was inside her. She laid back and could not move and he was a horse trailing the field ablazing an unseen path so blind with rage he had evolved to a car so hot with speed the engine burst. His seed burst and inside her he laid with his voice as sound and noise.

Nini rose and went to the bathroom returning for her clothes. She went to Abdullah's bedroom and his wife awake: What is it? A car speeding down the street braked reversed and the door slammed. Then steps to an unknown house. I want to tell you that yr husband was in bed with me. A door slammed and the night fell back to its mystery and secret. Abdullah loves me. I love him. Was it an imaginary bird that fell against the window dead from an empty sky? But.. She turned and walked out the house and up the street, nothing more pregnant than the feeling of loss. So lost a forest of tigers and beasts of our world caged the movements of possible travels of moving self. All motion blocked and guaged it was a wall so high the eyes could not see. So high, it was filled space of darkness. So high, the self was trapped in feeling. So stifled voice and words were lost. A taxi to home and warmth.

Nini sitting in a restaurant with Abdullah and Jabu eating food that brought her up. The place is beautiful, a feeling of transformed growth and a culture sliding through time manifest on the walls of the place. It is Saturday and the street is jammed with people who now repossess their lives trapped in a week of daily discipline and the rising through cold and rain. There is joyous noise and the hippies troop into the restaurant tasting the food that could release their fears. This is good, man. This is really good.

The black girl dressed in African clothes is a pillar of sullen feelings. she sweats and moves so fast. Her face unsmiling Nini watches her, this unselfconsciousness to the clothes of her wearing. Free and without feelings of strangeness. Another girl who like Isis, tightly covered in a wrap of ancient thread sits behind a stall selling artifacts of a regenerating past. The record shop next door sings with the music of her land and Nini longed to dance. The young black boys are expressing depth of feeling in the simple movements that express a logic of its own. The pulse of Africa moved to the Caribbean now shifted to a land of snow possess the air. Nini sees everything and silently her blood runs fast. Everything so live it is a threat to her being. Yet dance awakens in her blood then chilled by potential release.

She pays the bill and the men sit with talk. It is good this feeling and the slow rise of confusion. But she buys herself. The self being bought back after years of estrangement. Hippies in the street and the drums of Hari Krisna resounding in the air. The young black men laugh. "Dem blood clath white people do anything to feel." Nini laughs nervously and led by Jabu goes to the stall where the girl wrapped in a jelaba her big black eyes piercing through the corners of her head and her teeth so large and bright stands a perfect image of an African goddess save the cold paleness of her skin. Nini touches and holds the material in her hands and so beautiful she is moved. So touched by colour and designs conceived with purest feeling. She is moved.

So moved Jabu's fingers in her cunt stroking the arrow of emotion and Nini's controlled mass of flesh possessed now by feeling. Come in. Come in. Jabu's fingers wet with slim and her body emotes with intense feelings he plunges in. Herself is given and she lays dead upon the bed.

continued on pg. 57

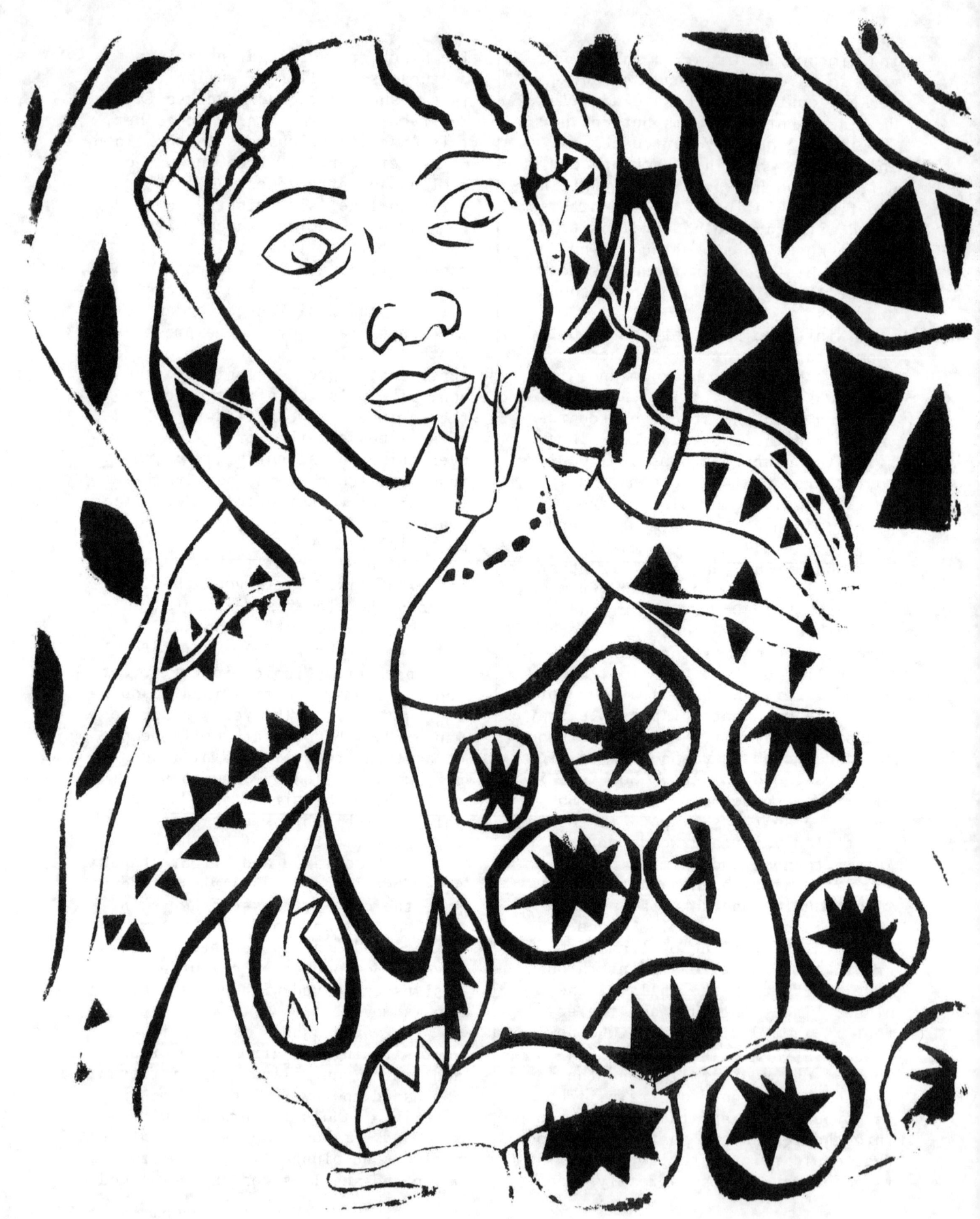

THE MEDITATORESS

Presenting— DINDGA McCANNON

Dindga McCannon was born in Harlem, U.S.A. The only girl, the only child and an energetic Leo to boot. She attended Fashion Industries High School until she was asked to leave for failing art. From there she went to Commerce High instead of where she really wanted to go: Art and Design. (She would have been left back a year and she says she thought school was alright and everything but not that alright.)

She's a painter, a printmaker, a lithographer, illustrator, jeweler, dressmaking-designer, and author. She's one of the few young contemporary black artists who has been able to make a living almost solely from her work. She's worked in factories, offices, shops, etc., when times were hard, but for the most part she's been able to earn her living from her creations.

Recently, she added author to that long list. Her children's book, *Peaches* which she wrote and illustrated was recently published by Lothrop-Lee Inc. She has also illustrated four other books, *Sati, the Rastifarian, Omar at Christmas, Children of Night*, written by Edgar White, *Speak to the Winds; Proverbs from Africa* by Kofi Opoku to be released soon.

One day I dropped by to purchase a painting. As I looked around her small gallery-apartment, while sipping tea and looking at her work, many questions came to my mind:

Nikki: Dindga, what have been some of the major problems confronting you as an artist?

Dindga: Money. Then every artist needs time, lots of time to explore themselves. However, it takes years to get to a point where you can support yourselves from your art alone and every hour spent on a 9 to 5 job is time taken away from your art and the exploration process. In the process of my development I HAD to go to work, that meant every morning

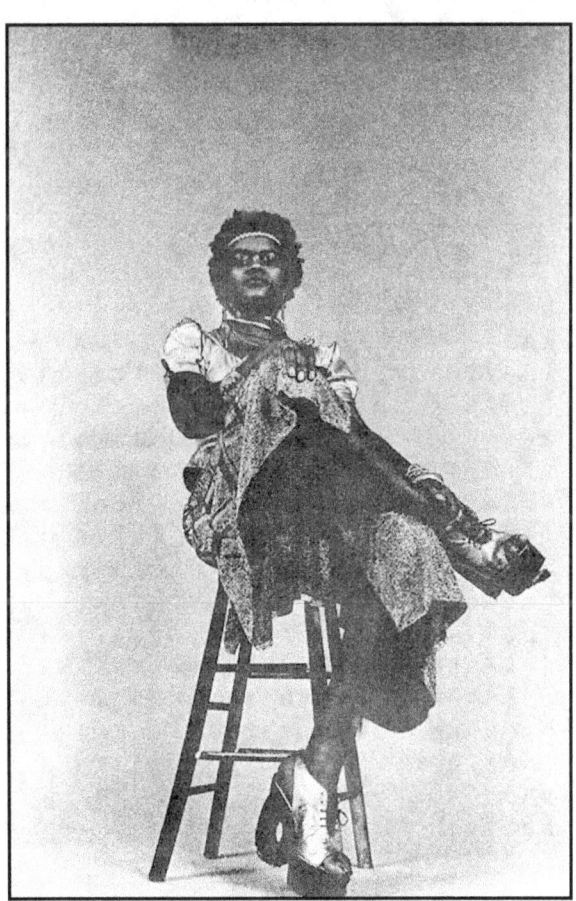

that I rose ('cept Sunday, Saturday I was working at work or working at home on all the things I couldn't do during the week) I had to live through twelve hours before I am able to do what is my expression. By that time, if my mind had survived the bland colors of the office or the factories, my body had just about had it. Exposure, rather lack of it, is another problem. If only ten people know your work, maybe two of them will purchase something once, perhaps three times. Exposure in the art world determines where you're going to show and the prices of your work. Winter is one of my personal obstacles. I hate it! It takes away the source of my energy, the sun. It also takes away employment for many artists. Those great temporary jobs teaching kids are gone, the outdoor shows have vanished, mural painting ceases.

Nikki: Do you think artists should marry or hook up with other artists, rather than someone with another completely different vocation?

Dindga: Not necessarily, cause artists are men too. They're men first, sometimes they're worst. There might be a lot of jealousy and unwholesome competition with one another. They need a helper too (laughs). Someone who'll cook, clean, get their clothes together, while the artist is into his or her art. But, an artist SHOULD be able to marry or hook up with another artist because, because you'd be on the same vibrating vibration and UNDERSTANDING would be heavy.

Nikki: For centuries men have put their art first and foremost. Is that how you feel about your work?

Dindga: I would hate to weigh my work against a human being. It is my oldest lover and I do love it. Anyone who would try to intercede in this affair can't be about positivity. Like when I arise in the morning I go to work. I keep working till it is absolutely necessary to go out. Then I come back. If my voyage out into the other world has not consumed all my energy, I work. If it has, I rest, then arise and work.

Nikki: I wonder how many housewives would like to have that kind of freedom--the freedom to be something other than a housewife or in addition to being a housewife.

Dindga: Like I said before they often have to make a choice between marriage and that something else. If they manage to do both they should consider themselves very, very lucky. But see, anything you want to do or be, YOU got to get on out there and try it. It's a drag to spend a whole lifetime wishing, never gaining courage to DO.

Nikki: Do Blacks have a special "school" that young Black artists emulate?

Dindga: Black art is a combination of various schools or methods. To me Black art is a visual music, it's by the people, for the people. The "school" can be anything from realism, to cubism, to surrealism. There are many Black artists who are trying to establish their own schools by

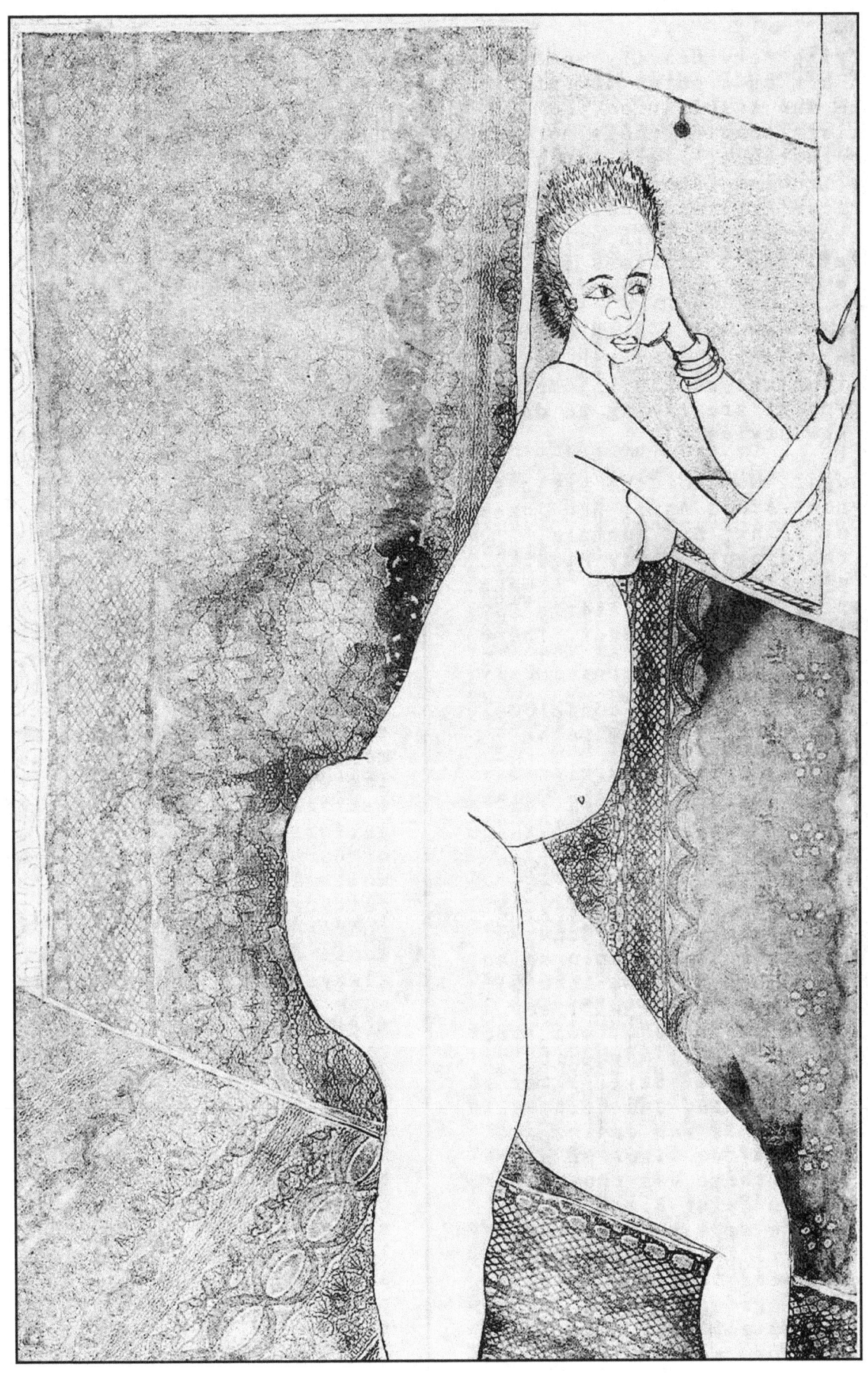

relying very heavily on African art as a point of reference and inspiration. Some artists combine their methods. For instance, I use African art, cubism (another form of African art) and realism in my work. And people will give it all kinds of names for lack of a formal one.

Nikki: Who if any of the young Black artists in using African art as their jumping off point are trying to develop new styles?

Dindga: Most of the artists I know--Addul Aziz, Ben Jones, Carol Blank, Dr. Ademola, Faith Reingold, Andy Pigatt, Otto Neals, Kay Brown, Akweke, Charles Abramson, Valerie Maynard, Stephanie Weaver. There are many more.

Nikki: Do artists consciously try to establish new techniques and styles?

Dindga: Things new are the result of an artist's exploration of the span of their imagination. Some artists sit down and deliberately try to discover new things. Others, in the process of exploration, stumble upon or work into a style. Then people will say that artist is mad. Then later on they say well maybe it might be valid. Still later it gets recognized and becomes in vogue. When I was coming up there were two kinds of Black artists--there was those who wanted to Paint Black or die and there were those who wanted to sell their work. The buyers were mostly white. So the last group painted white folks and got over that way. Once I knew an artist who exhibited in his gallery every

year. I told him he should remember his folks and paint some of us. The next year, all his paintings were Black subjects. Usually he would sell out, this time, he sold one piece. Things are changing somewhat but still not enough Blacks are buying our art. There are enough Black people with money to buy work but it's a matter of rearranging priorities.

Nikki: What kind of "campaign" do Black Artists have to wage to get more Blacks to buy their art?

Dindga: It has to be a constant, out and out campaign. One of the things I do is have all kinds of prices from one dollar up on my work so that everybody can afford to own SOMETHING of mine. For instance, I make cards which are sold reasonably through which more people can become familiar with my work. Black artists can rarely depend upon galleries for a complete way of earning a living, which white artists do. It's about getting yourself exposed beyond the gallery circuit because the same people almost always go to galleries. It sure would be nice to see one fifth as many people at any Black art show as come to see a Stevie Wonder concert (laughs). Another way to extend out into the Black community is through illustrating books. Books are considered commercial but that doesn't mean a fine artist has to be limited to doing commercial art. I have been able to express myself in my illustrations as I have been able to do in my painting. You know, even though most people can afford to buy a children's book, there still aren't enough Blacks buying them. I don't know if it's because they don't realize how important it is to supplement what their kids get in school or...

Nikki: But isn't it mostly because of distribution problems that Black books don't sell?

Dindga: Yeah. And also the buyer usually picks what's selling or what will sell (fast), subsequently, they only pick well known authors. (You can be well known in the Black community and unheard of in the white.) Black bookstores usually don't have salesmen coming into them unless they are well known. Also most cannot buy on credit which limits their selections.

Nikki: Have there been times that you've regretted your decision to become and remain an artist?

Dindga: A very few. Less as time goes on.

Nikki: O. K. But if you had the opportunity to change that, would you?

Dindga: Well as far as regrets go, I've definitely had my share. But because of my art, I have had a lot of "fun" and good experiences. Once I vocalized my thoughts about quitting to a friend of mine and you know what he said? He said I was insane and I COULDN'T do that, the community needs me. You see I've been committed to art since I was a chile. Because of what my grandmother called a hard ass head, I could never seri-

ously give up art. Like I was telling you before, it's like an ole lover; you get mad and curse and stump your feet, but you ain't going nowhere. Sometimes I get a little sad when people come up to me and tell me how famous I am, how they see my work evry time they look up. Then I ask them if they would please lend me 35¢ so I can get home and they give me the is she or isn't she unsure look.

Nikki: So you use a central theme in your work or is it a combination of themes?

Dindga: A combination of themes. My first theme is Black is Heavy, another is views on the Black woman. I feel there is a need to expose the many sides of us cause there are so many different things to be seen. Another theme is togetherness, Unity, Hope, and Love. Sometimes I go into spiritual things as I did in the print, "Woman Alone With Her Spirits."

Nikki: How has the Where We At, Black Women's Artist Collective to which you belong been helpful to your career?

Dindga: Yes, it has in terms of finding out about exhibitions and in terms of having women artist friends to communicate with. Before Kay, Faith and I organized the group, I knew few Black women artists. Now I know about thirty.

Nikki: What are your hopes and expectations for your daughter Afrodesia?

Dindga: Well, people sort of expect her to be an artist. She at this point (at the ole age of 7) wants to be a veter-

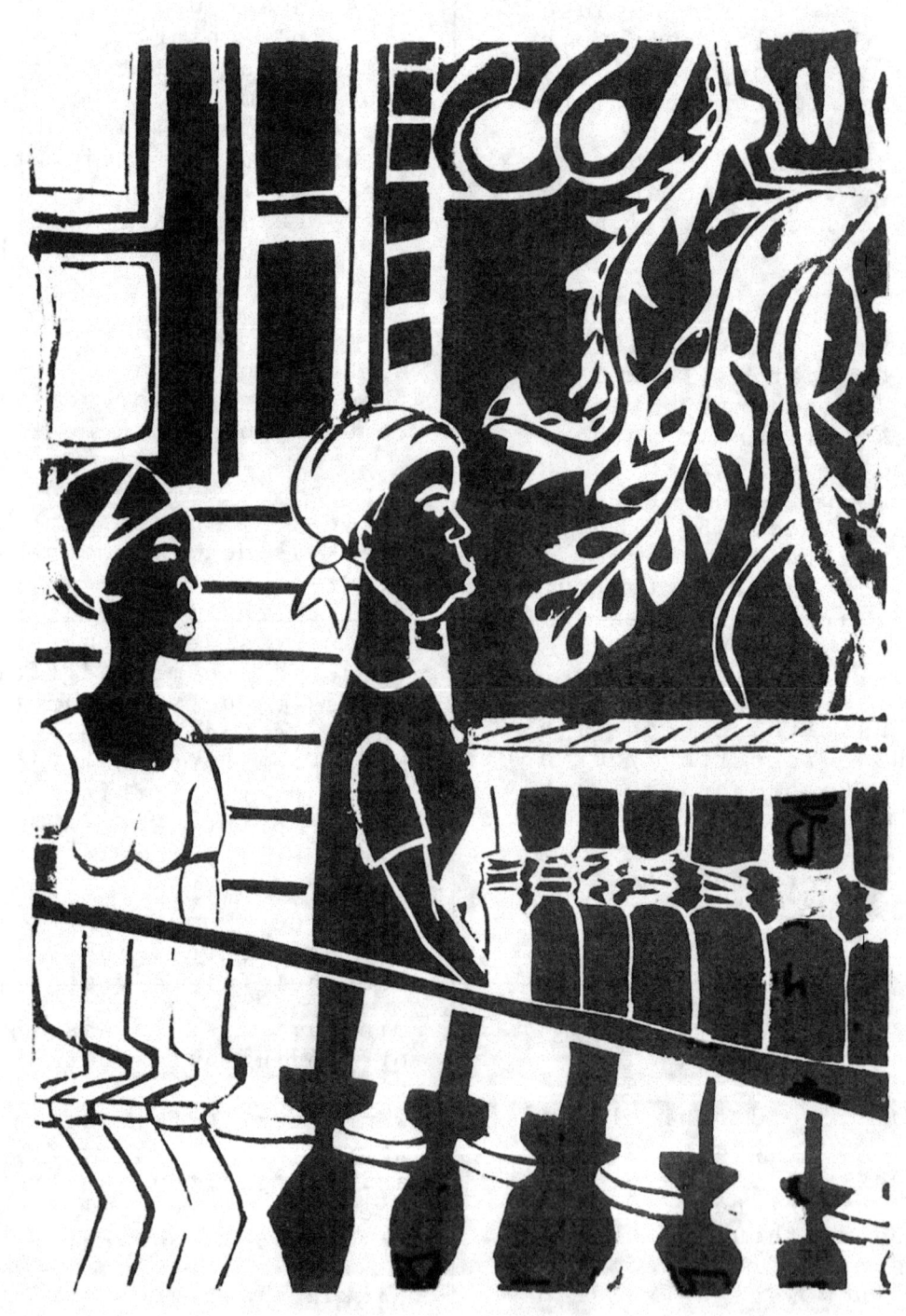

AT THE HOTEL ENCELSIOR

inarian. I want her to do whatever she wants to do long as it's legal and she can make a living out of it. It would be nice if she wants to be an artist, but not necessary.

Nikki: How did you happen to write a children's book?

Dindga: I've been writing ever since I was a kid. I was always encouraged to write by my teachers in school, mostly poems. Last year, one of the publishers I went to see about an illustrating job asked if I could write. I submitted a short story which was rejected, with a note attached to try to write something using my own experiences. So I started working on *Peaches*. It went through several revisions--from a group of short stories to a 125 page novelette. By that time the people who had published Ed White's books heard of my book and expressed an interest in seeing it. During the time I was writing *Peaches* I felt very schizophrenic because I would be writing one day, painting or printing the next. Finally I had to tackle one project at a time. Ed told me I could do it, but I was really surprised, amazed to see something of mine published. Mostly because I didn't plan or think about it until the book was half-way finished.

Nikki: Why do you have a reputation for your prints more so than your paintings?

Dindga: Because prints are less costly, for one thing. Another thing is my paintings are very bold and bright and some people don't like five thousand colors coming off the

wall. Also space is a problem for most of my paintings are large whereas my prints are much smaller and can fit anywhere. Then too, I don't exhibit my paintings because the gallery may not have the space and sometimes it is a real hassle transporting paintings.

Nikki: What type of person were you as a child and young adult?

Dindga: I was an average child except that I was constantly drawing, writing poems, reading every fairy tale written and I had an unquenchable thirst for monster movies and science fiction. As a young adult, some people who knew me then say I was always ahead of my time. I used to do lots of unconventional things in that period, not to be weird, but trying to find myself. Like when I was in Fashion High, we came to school dressed down every day. When I left there, I found freedom at Commerce cause no one was really concerned about things like that. I used to hang out in the Village, thinking all artists had to be beatniks (remember that word?). My wardrobe consisted of sweatshirts, sneakers, raggedy jackets and ole lady shoes. Then I discovered sandals. Not having a job, I had to ask my mother for some money to buy some. She, not believing in sandals, refused. So as usual, I became resourceful, at times of need. I took my sneakers, cut across the toe part, cut out the sides, bound the edges with some old leather trim and Voila! I had me some sandals. (When my mother saw them she forgot what she said and gave me the money.) I was always

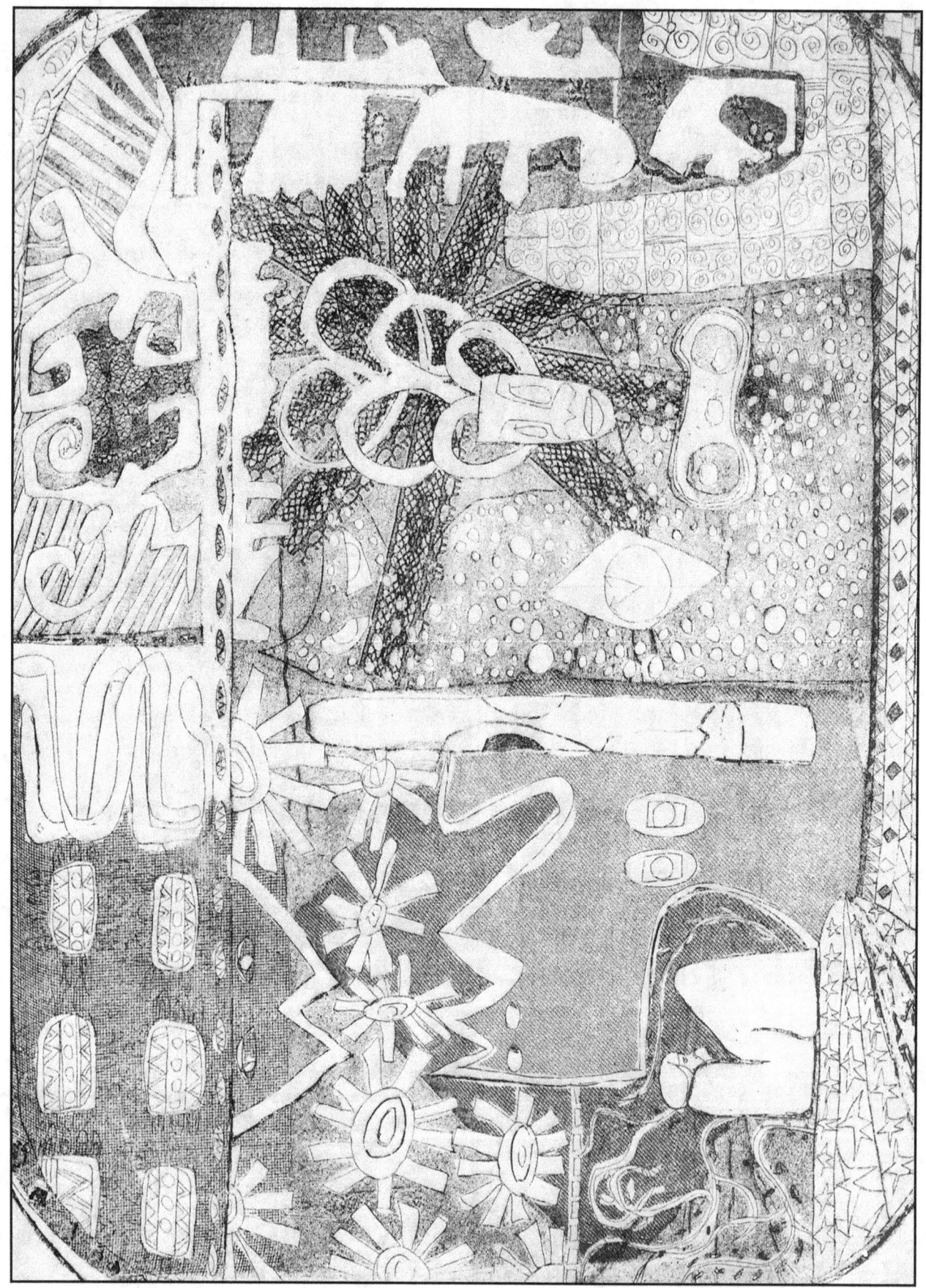

WOMAN ALONE

38

making something; collages, cakes, plays, crocheting, knitting, embroidery. I was very much a loner, mostly because, as an only child, I was alone a great deal and I really enjoyed it most of the time. Then the friends I had were just not interested in museums, plays and walking along the river. That's mostly what I did when I was out. At home I spent many hours locked up in my room, radio blasting, bellowing out some R & B while I was daydreaming or reading. I read everything I could get my hands on.

Nikki: What advice can you give Black adolescents about becoming artists?

Dindga: Well, I would tell them to get the tools of the trade, like drawing, together. They have to decide that this is what they really want to be about. Then try and never give up even when the whole world seem like it's shaky. Find yourself some Black teachers. Distractions come in many disguises, so beware. If possible, learn something which you can do to make a living while you're getting it together. Learn how to frame, some plumbing, etc. Artists like to live in lofts and it helps if you can fix it up yourself. Travel anywhere where you can. Seeing other lands and other people is mind-blowing and expanding. Most of all they have to learn patience because it's hard to live solely off one's art and the period of apprenticeship varies from 5 to 20 years, depending on the person. Lastly, live in peace (what comes around, goes around), and love your family even if they don't think being

an artist is hot stuff. My mother always told me, you can go to the top of the world but in the end it's your family who love the real, inner you and when the shit gets nasty, most Black families will help you, even when your name is mud.

Nikki Coleman is a writer, playwright and poetess and also an actress. She has appeared in an African ritual play called "Shango De Ina" with the JuJu Players; in a West Indian play, "Iron Band," at the Henry Street Theatre; "Fish and Chips" by Walter Jones at the Billy Holiday Theare; a Puerto Rican play called "The Junkies Stole the Clock." She is currently working on a play on male-female relationships called "How Many Ways Can You Skin A Cat?"

Pat Davis is a renowned Black woman photographer. She has exhibited with the Where We At Black Women Artists and all over the U.S.A.

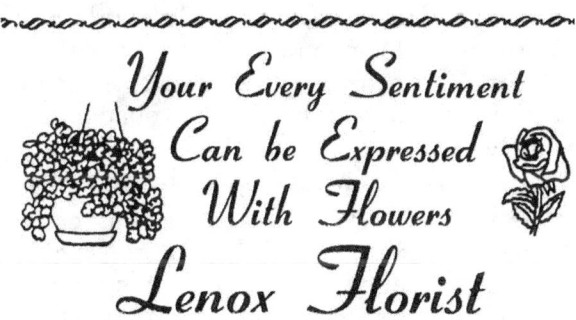

Poisons & Our Bodies

by Brenda Bailey

In my first article I dealt with why nutrition is important for survival and of course developing the right attitudes about food. Now, before I get down with the proper eating habits and healthy foods, I want to deal with certain substances that are poisonous to our systems and why they are poisonous. Before we can learn the correct eating habits to nourish and cleanse our bodies we must stop certain practices that are slowly killing us. The biggest killers in the black community are cigarettes, drugs, meat, and sugar.

Cigarettes are so very bad for the body, and have so many detrimental effects that I don't know where to begin. When one lights a cigarette and inhales the first puff, a chain of reactions begin that do a whirlwind of damage. After smoking for any period of time, the person is prone to sores on the mouth, especially in the corners which tend to be very dry and cracked. Also on the insides of the mouth little sores might appear which if not checked could lead to skin cancer. This condition on the internal and external areas of the mouth are caused by an element in the tobacco that is destructive to skin tissue & cells.

Cigarettes and smoking contribute to many other diseases and cause many deficiencies. Cigarette smoking is related to low blood sugar "hypoglycemia." It stimulates the production of adrenal hormones which causes blood sugar to be increased, thereby giving the needed "lift;" but insulin is quickly secreted causing the sugar level to fall again. One cigarette uses up to 25-35mg of Vitamin C, so the amount of Vitamin C is greatly reduced in the body. The main damage done by smoking seems to be that non functioning scars take the place of normal cells. This has a special effect on the lungs because a build-up of these scars would diminish normal cells and the lungs breathing capacity. This also takes place in the arterial walls, which could lead to arteriosclerosis. So the thing to do is to stop smoking immediately and start taking Vitamin C and E daily. I might also add, smoking also contaminates everyone's lungs that comes into a room where cigarettes are being smoked. Dangerous huh! Our lungs have a difficult enough time trying to breathe in all this pollution; it doesn't make sense to add to the problem.

Drugs are the next heaviest poison infiltrating through the Black communities. Whatever manner it is taken into the body it is detrimental to health. We must remember who we are as a race and where we are. We are a black race living in a white society. Now I'm sure everyone knows must of the stuff that is sold on the streets, in the speak-easies and after-hour joints is not heroin or cocaine, it is mainly some other chemical agent which is highly poisonous to the body. What is really shocking is that there is little thought to those dirty filthy syringes. I mean again there is the situation: the person is injecting numerous poisons into his/her bloodstream and then contaminating his skin and arteries with a needle that is more dirt than anything else. Disease is widely spread among users of these drugs. Another detrimental effect of the drugs are that they contaminate the blood and destroy the arteries leaving numerous scar tissue, which leads to poor circulation. I'm sure you've seen addicts and ex-addicts whose hands are swollen and puffy, this is because the veins and arteries have been damaged to the point where normal blood circulation is impossible. I was told by a doctor friend that it takes up to three & four years for the body to rid itself of the drugs completely. Drugs are bad in so many ways they completely alter the nervous system; they have such an effect on the liver it cannot function properly while being pumped full of chemical poisons-DRUGS. I don't think I have to really get into the effects it has on the mind, it takes the user completely out of focus with reality, in fact so far out that he loses touch with himself.

Meat, of course, is a food that that there has been a lot of controversy over. For centuries it was believed that we as human beings needed a certain amount of protein to function as normal, healthy, strong entities. Now I have learned the contrary, as a child meats were always a source of tension for me because I really disliked meat and my folks were always forcing me to eat it. I started realizing in my early teens, that those times I did eat a little meat my body felt sluggish and I felt as though I had some kind of dead weight in my stomach, a type of heaviness. After years of study and understanding the physiology of the body and the basics of nutrition, I know that meat is not necessary. I am not about to argue the case against meat but I am going to present the facts and permit the reader to judge for him/herself.

The erroneous theory that the body needs high-protein foods has done more harm than any other modern nutritional theory. Meats as a protein food act as a stimulation

for a certain time because they decompose at once in the human body into poison. I'm sure everyone knows that any kind of animal substance turns to a poisonous state as soon as it enters after oxidation with the air, especially at a temperature as high as the human body. Again we have numerous poisons (mucus & pus) entering into the bloodstream. Meat in itself contains numbers of germs and bacteria which infect the intestines causing colitis and cancerous conditions. Not to mention the harm caused by the new industrialization of meat, fish, and egg production. Now, we are dealing with a strained and diseased metabolism in the animals, and what is more shocking; an incredible amount of toxins, antibiotics and pesticides. A well of poisons to disturb normal body functionings appears in meat.

In addition excessive amounts of uric acid in the body is caused by meat-eating. Uric acid is excreted from the urine under normal conditions, but where there is an excess or a stress situation uric acid is prevented from being changed into urea and passed from the body in urine therefore it accumulates in the body. As a result of this accumulation of uric acid we find <u>gout</u> being the number one disease and also <u>rheumatism</u>, <u>kidney stones</u> and <u>gall stones</u>.

It has also been proven that a high-protein meat diet increases the appetite and the intake of food altogether. This is in complete contradiction to the majority of slimming diets for they preach protein burns up fat and decreases the appetite. While on the other hand meat produces the most destructive habit of gluttony.

Especially if the body is already sick or ill, meat-eating will only make the condition worse, for it further clogs the body and prevents normal functioning. Also when the body is ill the food intake level should be lowered not increased, as meat tends to increase the apetite it should immediately be discontinued.

continued on pg. 60

····· knotted ·····

Twisted minds dance to twisted music
Body cells shit through ribs mouth
Men souls dribbling from their finger toe
Breath of creation
Strangling the generation of youth.
Ice water so hot
Hotter than hot water
Can recognise its own hotness.
Once upon a time
An ole story folk-teller
Tells the story on an ole obeah woman
Who used to live in a backyard
Near the broken bridge village.
Woman of obeahness
Used to sleep on a bed of snakes
And drink poison
And spit into a dragon's eyes
To look for the truth.
The house of moon-day
The day of house night
Bring messages to the
World of corruption.
Torch-light shining
Into the darkness of death
Death sees itself for the first time
Time of itself turns backward its time
Spirits gods beat drums and dance
In the bosom of no remembrance
Of life and death
Mad men try to untie
The knotted air
Turning the madness of
World civilisation.
The looser the knot gets
The more knotted it becomes
Within the knotted knot.

Frank John
New York
'74

Clifford Glover

(10 years old shot to death in the back by racist cop)

Another demonstration
of the reality
    that confronts us.
Will his message again
    be in vain?
again the, the Blackwoman
    has cried
  to her Blackman with
a heart filled mouth for
    the protection of
     her children,
again the Blackman has stood
    juxtaposed to the
    reality that plagues
     our communities.
Must we only demonstrate
    Blacklove
at cry'in time,
    bed time,
and fist rais'in time,
    with eulogies that
    sound like empty

platitudes echoing from the
    dense jungles
of Harlems across
    america.
where is our dignity
    now?
Yessss
    down below
over-shadowed by
    disgrace.

There were no
    white cops
at the funeral.
    But jus'
    wait till you git home.....

Zizwe Omowale Wa Naafua

Correction

Dear Editor:
    I would like to say what an honor it is to have been selected to be in the first issue of your fine magazine. I do hope that the periodical proves to be of great benefit to us all, and that we will see it around for years and years to come. It is greatly needed.
    I would like, however to clear up some misunderstood statements in the article on Sounds in Motion. Bernadine Jennings, a member of our dance company, teaches Horton Technique at the Sounds in Motion School. This dance style was devised by Lester Horton. James Truit and Thelma Hill are two of the foremost experts of this technique and Ms. Jennings received her training in Horton from both of them. In fact, she continues her studies with Thelma Hill at Clark Center. Alvin Ailey worked with the late Lester Horton and some of his early work grew out of the influence of the Horton style.
    Another error (in the article) involved the name Pearl Primus in connection with other leaders and innovators in the concert dance field.
    The Sounds in Motion School at 110 East 125th Street offers classes in modern dance, ballet, West Afrikan dance and dance for children. For further information one may call 534-9875.
    Thank you. Much success with Impressions.

Dianne McIntyre

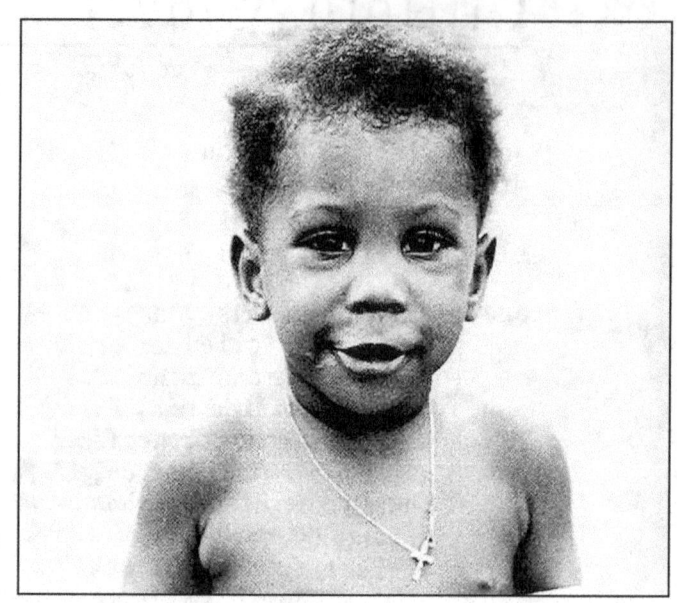

Bill Wilson

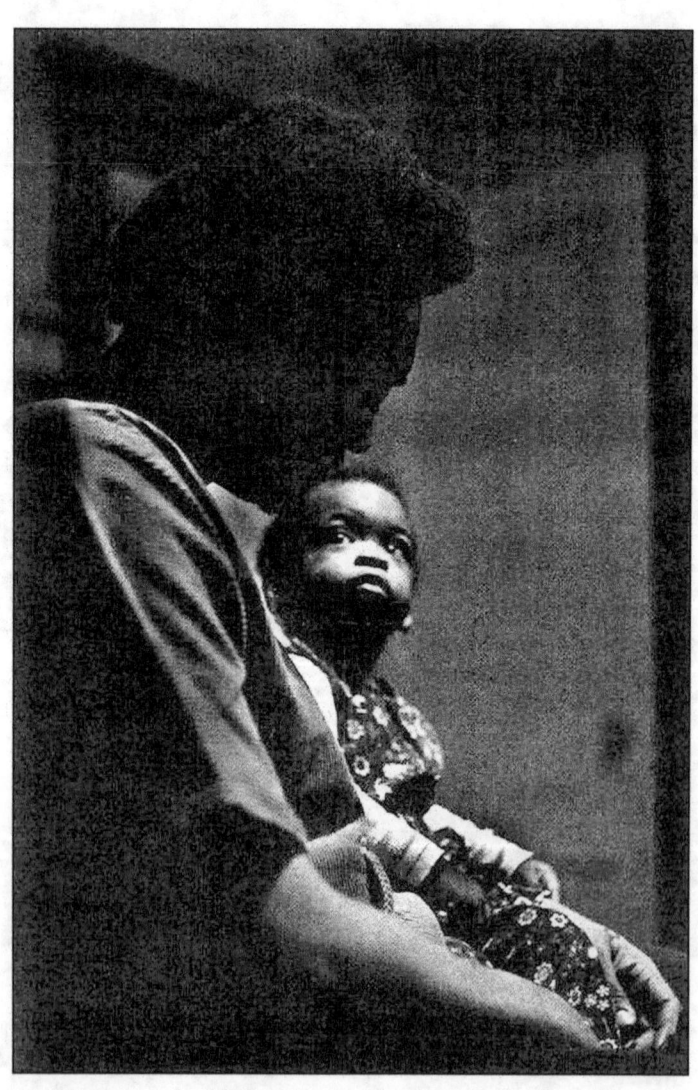

Ronald K. Gray

cause my father worked so hard-
he was always gone.

Hector: What did he do for a
living?

Bill: For a while, he started
out as a great baratone singer;
he was also a song writer and
he came along when there was
just nothing for black people.
He worked for people like Bes-
sie Smith, Ma Rainey; he was
during that Golden Period. As
a matter of fact, I was born
on the road. My mother was
Miss Negro America 1925 and she
was very pretty and made many
appearances. At one point, they
were tired and decided to set-
tle down. They tried to get me
into theater. I had no desire.
My mother tried to interest me
in reading. But they both had
an enormous influence on me
cause I grew up among adults.

Hector: So your activities
were primarily with them when
you did hang out?

Bill: Yes. Also older cousins-
older people.

Hector: What kind of effect do
you feel this had on your whole
development?

Bill: Well, I don't know. It
was very strange because those
people were quieter; it seemed
to be where I belonged. I never felt as though I was out of
step. I always hated games,

running around in the streets.

Hector: ...Because that was
stupid?

Bill: No, it just didn't get
me. Well sometimes I used to
try, I'd go to play ball. Then
I went out for the track team.
I was very good, I was very fast.

I realized I could run better if
I ran cross-country, so I did
that for awhile but it didn't
excite me. The only thing that
I really enjoyed was drawing; I
drew really well and I won a
scholarship but I got kicked out
of school.

Hector: So you didn't go to
college and all that stuff?

Bill: No. I used to hate it, I
used to regret that I didn't?

Hector: Why?

Bill: You see, all my friends
went to college and I'd come
back to Philadelphia to go to
the Penn Relays and see them all
and they'd talk about being away
at school and I was working.

Hector: What kind of work did
you do?

Bill: I was working in a leather factory, which was not
what I was supposed to be doing.
The stench got so raunchy in
the summer that I had to quit.
Then I worked for a Medical School, which was the worst job
I've ever had. We just couldn't
get decent jobs. I mean, the
ads in the paper said BLACK
PEOPLE NEED NOT APPLY, so we
used to get all the junk: the
mailroom, drumming orders at
luncheonettes and stuff like that.

Hector: As a middle class black,
how did the color problem when
you were growing up really effect you?

Bill: Very much. All blacks
got through the same thing on
the same level. I think that
middle class blacks tend to
know it more but they won't
admit it, but they know. You
know the poorer black is str-

iving to get that house, to get that car in the garage and all that. But the middle class black has it but he still knows that something is missing. My parents still had to deal with me coming home from school with all kinds of racial insults from teachers, being beat up in the streets by white kids, being insulted at white supermarkets, being shoved around by the police.

Hector: What did that do to you?

Bill: After awhile you knew that that's what was happening. You know, I've seen it in Movies where it destroys the child, but it kind of makes you stronger. You stop trusting them at a very early age.

Hector: Where in Philly did you live?

Bill: West Philly.

Hector: Wasn't it crazy around that time?

Bill: No. We were like the 2nd black family in the neighborhood, they were all white. My next door neighbor was white and they didn't, wouldn't speak to us-of course. So we were sitting there isolated and then about 10 years into that, the Communists came into the neighborhood. They would set up store-fronts and they'd try to figure some way to get Middle Class blacks in, so they would give these little dances at night- turn on those bright lights and turn up the music and have these interracial couples dancing in the light so that you could see it. They were trying to get you to come in. They were really smart. When your stomach is full you think about your head. It's part of the American myth that when you reach middle class status that you no longer understand-that you're insensitive.It's not true. If you're black it doesn't matter.

Hector: What was your first break into film as a writer/director?

Bill: My first thing was a movie called Stop and that's what it did, it was never released.

Hector: How did you get to write Ganja & Hess?

Bill: Kelly Jordan called me in to write a film; he said don't be embarrashed because it's a horror film. The first black horror film; it's going to be dynamic; it's going to be fabulous and I'm embarrashed to say it to you. And I started to say, you should be...so he invited me to write it.

Hector: Was it an original story?

Bill: Well, they came up with some ideas, they had had a script first written by a very good filmmaker and writer...but it wasn't exactly right so they said, well come up with a script and any ideas that we might want to buy. So he said, have you done any film and I said, well yes I have. I just finished directing a film called Stop that wasn't released and also there was a cut of my cut of Stop. So I took him over and showed him Stop. After seeing it he asked me to direct it also, so I did.

Hector: Initially did they give you full control of the film?

Bill: Well, yes; I had full control. I think they had another film done in advance and they were having trouble with that and so all the producers were way over there dealing with that, so I was left alone.

Hector: What happened after it was finished, wasn't there some problems?

Bill: The thing that really prevented me from going off on myself for having done it in the first place because at the time Ganja & Hess got no support from audiences. White writers were writing pieces on it but no black writer wrote anything. Finally Paul Carter Harrison wrote a piece in Players Magazine and I think Clayton Reilly wrote a piece. Black writers weren't writing about it and we really needed our Black audiences at that time.

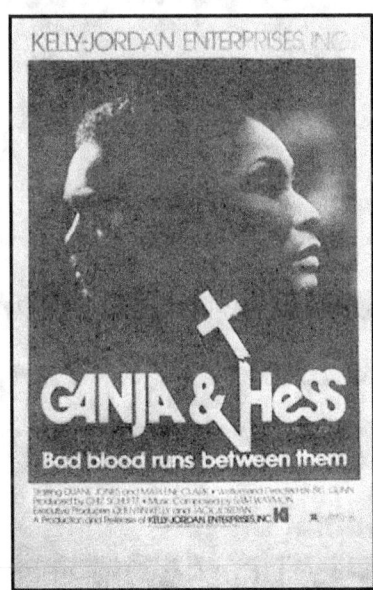

Hector: Well, why do you think that was? I mean we admittedly know that that point around '69 Cotton Comes To Harlem, into the 70's and with all those types of films were coming out and very definitely no one was ser-

iously making Black Films; they were making commercial films and what was coming out was pretty much trash. Now here you are 1971/1972 attempting to do a serious kind of thing, perhaps a personal kind of film and nobody deals with it. Why not?

Bill: Well, I think it had never happened before from a Black director so they weren't ready for it and they (studio) didn't have the money to exploit it. So nobody knew about it & they stuck in the Playboy Theater and they saw it as a ART FILM-and you know Blacks aren't necessarilly on 57th street at night. So they only had enough money to keep it there for 7 days. The next thing I know is that I went Cannes with it and that's the thing that really saved me-stopped me from going out on myself. It was incredible, the reception that the film got there. It was very strange, I mean they were really dealing with the film. Because you know commercial Black films don't sell over there. Shaft ran for a month in Paris and closed. It was insane, incredible.

Hector: What was there about it that really appealed to them?

Bill: Well you know Jean Cocteau is their most adventurous filmmaker, in terms of the mind. This is what was about him, he kept coming out with films that were surreal.

Hector: I see...like totally removed from those action rock-'em, sock 'em f--k 'em films. I understand that you were hired to do the film but philosophically why did you decide to treat the vampire like you did?

Bill: Well first thing, I don't know what print you saw (ED.NOTE.)

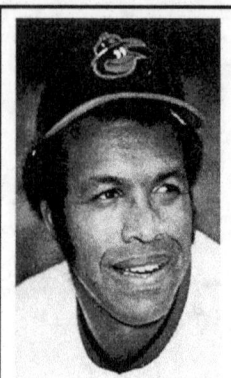
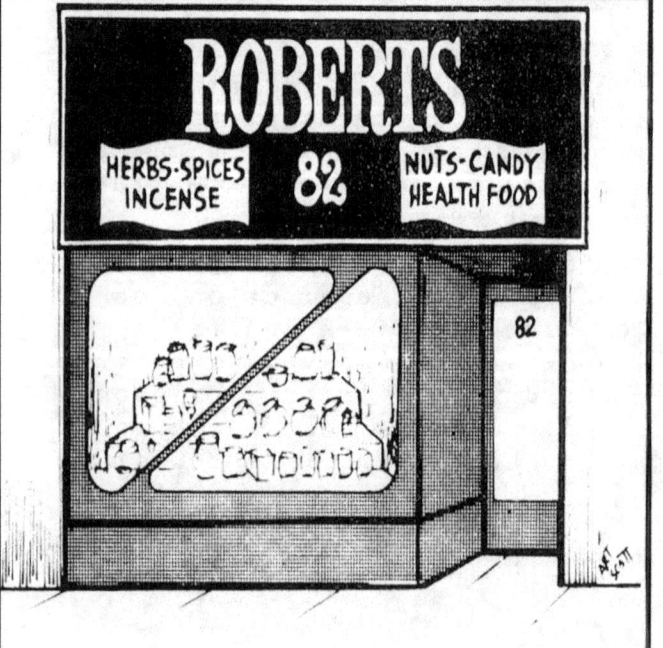

There are more than one print, Bill's original cut and another that was later cut by the studio.)

Hector: I saw the one at the Countee Cullen Library.

Bill: Well..an interesting scene was cut out from this last one that we saw at the Countee Cullen Library. Where he says to her, "You don't mind me being this way, being strange or whatever," after she found out that he killed her husband. She says, "Well no, because everybodies some kind of freak." Well I always saw him, my character...because finally my character emerges as Alexander in the Black Picture Show. I saw the character trapped in a vampire movie. I saw this man come to life in my typewriter and in my own mind. Literally, I kept trying to move him from one situation to the other within the script-I was writting the script. I realized that I always had to function within the horror film. I saw Duane now wandering through this horror film trying to find his way out and when I look back to see what it's all about, that's what it's really all about, it's a much more interesting character who is trapped into a trivial situation.

Hector: Do you really see the genre of horror as trivial?

Bill: Well, I'm not really interested in Horror- I'll tell you why. It doesn't interest me. It used to frighten me when I was a child. But. since I understood it, it no longer frightened me-when I found out what it was all about.

Hector: Well, what is it all about?

Bill: Sex.

Hector: That's the vampire's trip...?

Bill: Yes, it's also, you know ...there are girls being carried away in night gowns, being carried into the woods. You know what that phantasy is all about...I mean, what happens when they're caught. Also it's bodies stripped of their souls, quilt and everything. If you figure out the phantasy and you're still fascinated with it, then you're truly theirs-in a sense. So after I found out what it was all about, it stopped frightening me, because as a child I couldn't even look at a picture of the thing. That was because I didn't know what it was all about. When I found out what it was all about I couldn't care less.

Hector: You mentioned at the Countee Cullen Library that blood represents truth in the film...

Bill: I was trapped into that in a sense-I trapped myself into that. It had to represent something. I mean you can't make a movie with gore all over the place and actually make it about blood... so I had to replace it with something.

Hector: For yourself?

Bill: That's right. So I took something rather obvious, that I thought people would know what that meant. I realized that I couldn't use money because then it would be just two floozies running around trying to find money. So all this is a trap, if I didn't do this I wouldn't have

continued on pg. 52

from audience: That's a lie, he wasn't invited; we came to ask you why he wasn't invited.) (Others in the audience drown out the protestors, urging Askia to continue, "Read on Brother.") It's alright. It's good to have a little fire.

I'm just going to go briefly into the revolutionary journals. Ed Spriggs back there,(indicating to the audience) Bro. Muhajir, Marvin X, all kinds of beautiful, veteran writers, Sis June Jordan, I think Sara Fabio is here somewhere in the audience, anything you or the people want to add is fine. But, what I'm relating to you is what I have lived, what I have seen with these eyes. When this movement originally began, there was no such thing as cultural nationalism. The movement, the nationalism, was revolutionary, and the culture & politics interrelated with and complemented one another. The young people who developed this movement were searching to define themselves within America. While they respected Dr. King, they did not agree with his theory that we were citizens denied our rights. It was only after reading Bro. Harold Cruse's article "Revolutionary Nationalism and the Afro-American in 1963 in Studies in the Left that they began to see themselves as colonized people. Parallel to that, Black America, the ideological journal of RAM, the REVOLUTIONARY ACTION MOVEMENT, also developed the dual-nation thesis, the fact that we were a colonized nation within a nation; the fact that the Americans brought the Africans here and colonized the Africans within the south, within the metropolitan country. The thesis of that was that the primary contradiction in this society is all of white America versus Black America, in other words, the national question which does not mean we are pro-capitalist. From the beginning we were anti-capitalist. It was not even a question of socialism, and anyone who was involved knew this (applause) because the world is only divided now, in terms of economics, between some kind of collective economy and exploitative capitalism, and Black people are not fools. But then again, maybe some of the cult figures were not studying these journals like they should have been. The Black Arts Movement Repertory Theatre School developed in spring 1965 after the death, after the martydom of A Hajj Malik al Shabazz in Harlem. It was a Pan-African Youth Conference sponsored by Muhammad Ahmad, the Field Chairman of RAM, RAM artist-activists, Larry Neal and Askia Muhammad Toure as Co-Chairmen, people like Queen Mother Moore, Jane Shabezz, Malcolm X's lieutenant, and Avery Spellman, the well known radical black critic. It was these forces who, working closely with the grassroots nationalist community, introduced Leroi Jones to the peoples' movement in Harlem. Harold Cruse was there; I think Bob Hamilton of Soul Book was there, and also Bro. Keorapetse Kgositsile, who was my roommate at the time. One of the problems in our movement uneven development. We've all had our contradictions; I don't want to use this to just castigate, but when you see people who have influenced a generation of young people by their image turn on those same young people and try to destroy them and berate them, that is hipocracy, that is hipocracy. I mean, if you are going to call somebody a reactionary nationalist, that's fine, as long as you have had a steady principled position. But, if you have trained and influenced these people, worked with them, read with them, etc, and then turn on them, your attitude is that of a traitor. So the movement was African collective. That's what is important. One of the contradictions we faced in Harlem was that the grassroots nationalist community was not sure about

the character of LeRoi Jones.
They jumped on Larry and me about,
the brothers like Elombe Braith,
one of the steadfast young Black
leaders in revolutionary nationalist culture, the brother of AJAZZ
naturally shows, which were instru-
mental in changing the consciousness of our sisters throughout the
early part of the movement. One
of the problems we had was when
LeRoi Jones came uptown to Harlem,
the Black Arts, and brought his
beatnik friends with him who were
smoking reefer all over the community. The community forces jumped
on us and said "we thought you
said this brother was together."
We started having seminars just
like we're having here, panel
discussions with the various artists involved in terms of the
roles of the artist and writer
in the Black community, and all
these Europeans were in the audience, at intimate programs where
Black people were discussing their
destiny. A revolt was led by
Larry Neal, Askia Muhammad Toure,
Harold Cruse and Bob Hamilton
against LeRoi Jones' bringing his
friends to Harlem. We confronted
him before the people, with the
people with us, and fights almost
broke out. We put the Europeans
out! We love the brother, but we
had to nudge him into Black consciousness because his contradictions were
glaring. (Multiple interruptions
from those in audience who resent
what has just been said about Jones--
Why didn't you open your mouth for
the last 10 years about this?) Brothers, I refer you to Black Dialogue
Magazine, Winter/Spring, 1967/1968.
(Where you been in the struggle for
the last 10 years man?) That's all
I want to say about that.

The movement was radical; it
was like a combination of politics
and culture interrelated. It was
radical; it had links international,
including Bro. Malcolm. One of the
things which set the movement back
terribly was in 1966 February, a
year after Malik's assassination,
Larry Neal, Askia Muhammad Toure,
several other radical writers, writing with Liberator Magazine. A
special Malcolm issue of Liberator
Magazine, projecting his image all
over the place. This magazine was
not only national but international.
Now the result of that was that the
power structure moved against the
radical political culture, collective
leadership of the Black Arts Movement.
Muhammad Ahmad was forced underground,
Askia Muhammad Toure was forced
underground, and Larry Neal was shot
down in the streets by agent provocatuers. It was in this interim period
that Life Magazine, June 1966, moved;
the power structure was moving not
only with provocatuers but also with
mass media to destroy the movement.
Life Magazine came out with an article " The Extremist: A Plot to Get
Whitey." Named in that article were
Baraka, Askia Muhammad Toure, Larry
Neal and Muhammad ahmad. who was
known as Max Stanford at that time.
About a year or so later, I believe
it was, Life Magazine again projected
Ron Karenga, who was at that time a
west coast leader, as national because the power structure deals on
more than one level. A gap had
been put in the political culture
movement, and it had to be filled.
They just make avenues, and people
take it on with their egos if
they don't have that particular
thing tohether. The gap was
filled and for the first time, as
a matter of fact from that time
on, we found that the political,
the national liberation struggle
which was Pan-Africanist, which
was socialist, which was anti-
capitalist, anti-imperialist,
was replaced by a reactionary
aspect of nationalism. Cult
figures emerged and developed,
and culture was separated from
the political aspect of the
struggle. For the first time all

across the country, cadres and masses of the people, etc., we heard the term cultural nationalism. That's where it came from. And, the problem, in terms of people who consider themselves socialists, is that often they don't do historical research in terms of their own movement. What has happened a lot, I think, in terms of people who are **socialist** pointed is that a lot of emotion was generated by conflict between us and the Panthers. As a result of this, the entire nationalist movement, including the revolutionary nationalists who were anti-capitalist and anti-imperialist, were also labled reactionary. I think it is of note that the cultural figures were also reactionary in terms of their treatment of our women, the sisters being repressed, the whole thing of walking into places and if a male walked in the sisters would have to pop to attention, etc. This was not the practice of the original political, cultural revolutionary nationalists because we are one with our sisters, and we agree with the statements of our Sis. Joyce Ladner and everyone that has said, that half a nation cannot liberate itself (applause). That's for those brothers who take the class position. We were not suppressors of women. We were anti-capitalist, anti-imperialist and remain to be, to this day!

With that said, I'm going to pull back and let the other brothers and sisters take it on from here. (Applause)

B. GUNN, *continued from pg. 49*

made the movie. So, if they had said...here's $300,000.00, go make a movie, I wouldn't have made a vampire movie.

Hector: Yes, because that's not your modality. What do you think should happen in Black films for Black people?

Bill: I know what Black people have been expecting in films. They really expect an education. One really shouldn't , because the film is always the results of someone's imagination. No matter how terrifically right it seems, it is still messed up in terms of you. This is what was going on the the other night and a lot of the questions I wouldn't answer because they wanted very specific things from films so that they can apply it to their lives and take out and try to deal with that but it's very wrong because you have to look at where it's coming from. Because sometimes it's coming from very warped vision, which is not necessarily someone playing but thinks they're playing. Its like a Rorschach test; you're really out there throwing images right out of the mind. Which is very interesting if the audience can see it that way.

Hector: You mean like a guide for them..?

Bill: That's right. It must not be a guide for them. White people don't do that, I guess that's because they've had heroes for so long.

Hector: Yes, but they deal with that?

Bill: ...and our leaders keep telling us that this film has got to mean something to your life- that you should take this film home and apply it to their wife and their child and their future and education.Bull.

continued on pg. 56

R. WESLEY, *continued from pg. 8*

were publicly threatened with physical harm not very long ago if he gave an unfavorable review, or that sometimes the critic in question found himself agreeing with a white critic in his negative assessment of the work being reviewed and therefore bit his tongue and deliberately lied rather than take a chance on being branded politically unsuitable to view a Black play.

In questions regarding Art Vs. Politics, I say there is no dichotomy. It is my contention that art and politics *do* mix and that standards of excellence *must* be applied, otherwise we find ourselves playing the Black audience cheap. A bad play is a bad play and The Folks know it, having been exposed to the most sophisticated entertainment business in the world. No Blood who has paid $3.50 for a ticket to see a show in Harlem or Bed-Stuy is gonna dig seeing a play that is half-rehearsed or just plain poorly done. The same is doubly true of the Blood who may go down to Broadway and see a show for $12.50 and feel cheated.

Unlike the white critic, who merely sits back and judges a work on whether or not it is entertaining, the Black critic must decide whether or not the play is politically relevant, artistically sound and professionally done. He must address the play from reference points that are from inside the Black culture and he should be able to point out to any audience that cares to listen why such and such a play is worthwhile even though the so-called major critics dismissed it with a wave of their hands.

If there exists a crisis in criticism in the Black Theatre, it is because we have never given our critics as much attention as we should have nor have we seen to it that they have adequate and continuous access to the Black nation's collective minds. This situation must be corrected or else Black Theatre will always be doomed to being the prey of insensitive and uninformed white critics who have little knowledge of us and very often could care less.

Richard Wesley
February 16, 1975

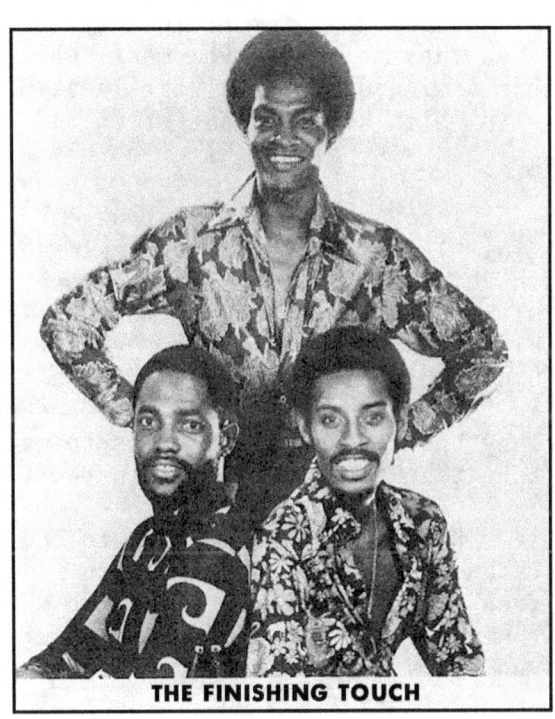

THE FINISHING TOUCH

Black people. He began travelling to Black townships and learning about Black life. Out of his exposure to this culture came his first play, No-Good Friday, which dealt with life in the Black townships. In South Africa, the mere association of a white with Blacks places even the white in danger of being persecuted, and Fugard was no exception. The anti-apartheid theme appears in all of his plays.

Every Black man and woman in South Africa has to carry a passbook, and must report to his township commissoner every 72 hours. The passbook situation is the theme around which Sizwe Banzi is built. In that play, the main character is forced to take on the identity of a dead man in order to defy the orders of the government, which has assigned him to a work location with which he is dissatisfied and which has separated him from his family.

The "curfew" and "influx control" laws (Blacks are not allowed in white areas after dark), along with the ruling that one must visit his township commissioner every 72 hours, hindered Kani and Ntshona in their efforts to meet with Fugard. They had to time their trips to make sure that they stayed within the law.

Kani and Ntshona bring to The Island a style of acting which is free of affectation. They give us themselves, men expressing themselves artistically to convey a message to the world about the way of life which their fellow Black citizens must accept. The synthesis of the experience of Kani and Ntshona as Black men in South Africa to the technique of Athol Fugard as a politically conscious white artist has resulted in powerful theater. When the two prisoners perform their scene from Antigone, the statement they are making about their own lives through art is equaled by the effectiveness of art in making their personal statement. Art becomes entirely functional, which is the basic concept behind the collaboration of Kani, Ntshona and Fugard in devising works to express the South African experience.

Lighting for The Island and Sizwe Banzi is Dead is by Ronald Wallace. Most of the time the lighting is dim, perfectly expressive of the depressing state of prison life. Scenic Design is by Stuart Wurtzel. The set is simple conveying the barrenness of the enviornment. Costumes are by Bill Walker, and the design consultant is Douglas Heap ✿

BLACK PICTURE SHOW

"Art without me is genocide at best." With this statement, Alexander, the protagonist of Bill Gunn's BLACK PICTURE SHOW, expressed the dignity and anger of many Black artists who must deal with the contradiction of trying to earn a living from their art in a materialistic society of false values. The pressure of such an existence is great; indeed, great enough so that, in the play, Alexander is to go mad shortly after making his statement of independence and self-determination. Forced by debts and a wife who is too accustomed to the bourgeois lifestyle with which Alexander has provided her to ever consider giving it up, Alexander finds himself forced to render himself available to a white Hollywood film producer. As a Black artist, he realizes he is copping out, and it is the pain of this self-betrayal which facilitates his madness.

Gunn presents the events which lead up to Alexander's breakdown as a poem to the artist's ability to withstand the pressures to sell out for as long as he has. Clearly, Alexander is motivated by a creative force which, in its embracing of the beauty of life in all its fullness, is in direct contradiction to the paranoia and sterility of the psychiatric unit in which the play is set. Like a poem, Alexander's madness progresses along a delicate pattern which can only be totally understood by being read to the end. His encounters with other people--his son, J. D., a director of rip-off Black films; Rita, Alexander's second wife, who indulges with him in games of manipulation; Norman, a companion who wants to help Alexander out of his madness; and the producer and his wife, who see their dealings in Alexander's future as a pleasant evening's diversion--are all informed by the need to make an impression on the person with whom he is communicating. Not just the normal impression of small talk and passing time, but an impression of Alexander's very essence, his identity not as a man who thinks of art as a hobby, but as a man who passionately wants to *live* his art and is constantly being frustrated in the attempt.

BLACK PICTURE SHOW functions not only as a discussion of the role of art in our society, but also as a metaphor for the state of Black people as living in a world which is dictated and dominated by white values and culture. One of the most striking images in the work occurs when Alex-ander's wife gets down on her knees to gather the thousand-dollar bills that the producer has arrogantly dropped on the floor. Of course, the power that the money of the dominant culture holds over the recessive culture can serve to keep the recessive culture in check (no pun intended), just as Alexander's ability to create is held in check by the necessity to create something which will have value on the market place. Any time that he spends creating work which cannot bring him money is time that is not being used to insure his physical survival, even though his mind is being used constructively.

In the recent production of BLACK PICTURE SHOW at Lincoln Center, jazz was integrated into the form of the play. Just off the set, Sam Waymon and five other musicians performed a score which Waymon wrote for the play, with lyrics for two songs, "Black Picture Show" and "I Feel So Good," written by Bill Gunn. This music gave the audience an entrance into Alexander's mind, a feel for the drives which moved the man and allowed his art to control his entire life and personality. Several times during the course of the play, Alexander opened the doors which separated the musicians from the ongoing stage action. When he asked them for an affirmation of a statement he'd just made, they said, "Yeah!" The music in his mind was the only thing keeping him in touch with himself.

In one of the arguments he has with his father, J. D. (whose name stands for "Jesus Delivvers") insists that the politics of revolution for Black people have been replaced by what J. D. terms the "politics of indifference." Thus, at the end of the play when Alexander is symbolically murdered by the producer and his wife, one might believe that compromise has been embraced as a solution to the artist's problems. However, in light of Alexander's resultant madness we must appreciate the total situation not as one of compromise but one in which the protagonist is presented as a victim. This implies not exclusively an acceptance of being a victim, but also the realization of being a victim as the first necessary step toward doing something about being a victim.

Dick Anthony Williams was excellent as Alexander, as was Carol Cole as his wife, Rita. Norman was played by Graham Brown. The producer was played by Paul-David Richards. Linda Miller played his wife. J.D. was played by Albert Hall. The scenery was designed by Peter Harvey. The costumes were designed by Judy Dearing. Lighting was by Roger Morgan.

Speech deleted from
BLACK PICTURE SHOW

Everything is the emergency, isn't it? You only decide to move when an emergency takes place, screaming this should have been done and that should have been donewhen everything that was done before was programmed to end in a crisis. You are crisis oriented. Then it becomes a life of patching, and when your lives are all patched up, then you use that as proof that the bureauracy can work. To you, the American, Hollywood, fantasy crisis is the only relevant plot. Then you force your fantasy into the reality of our lives. I can deal with your fantasy, but when you develope your fantasy into a game and we're herded up and pushed into that game...I was never poor, I infiltrated myself into the streets. I was turned out by hip black faggots, but I was careful enough to brush off what I didn't need. I took advantage of that to learn, to understand the true spirit of America. I learned that I must be a victim of it to be anything else is to be a part of the fantasy. I was able to support my art by selling drugs to rich white folks. THE COUNTER REVOLUTION.

(DELIVERED BY J.D. TO THE WHITE FILM PRODUCER)

B. GUNN, *continued from pg. 52*

It's too much responsibility. I mean it really is. I think that I'm a critical filmmaker I know I am, and that's my personal business. I don't do it because it's my duty. I do it beacuse I simply am black, I mean that's the reality of my existence, the only thing. Everything that I see or do up to this point has been political. When I get 70 I'll probably just go out there and wipe out the garbage...I don't know, I just might do that tomorrow morning. Even though it's political I would like for it to be looked at as a true poem about me.

continued on pg. 59

Only nights would see him and she entered another world. Nights would see her in strange houses and joints at her lips she inhaled to no heightening of an unmoved nervous system. Her world is closed and opened. Feeling heightened it would drop with a small understanding of its use. Use was her only weapon since she could not combat the weapons of their using. Her derangement under kiss of prolonged passion of unfeeling conditioned to seeing with distortion an amorphous mass in her brain. Even her child so gentle it was beyond their reaching. Even her ways and mode of speech so hated with intense feeling yet they were rooted to this use of her life. She could not see and moved more by pain she reeled under manipulating fingers. Open the womb of feeling. Give to men of seeking and of change.

Laura was convinced that she was mad. Convinced that she was destined to taste a fruit of slow change now blemished by its age. Nini had become the tape recorder of their mouths and would attack Laura's alienation and lack of faith. Laura so removed from anything that was organized was a being rooted to the most pessimistic vision of human beings.

Nothing could be seen simply as a mould or shape of words without the weight of existence manifest in the soul of feeling. Once actions transcended words vision is cleared of the debris of controlling stares. Move beyond words expressed without meaning to further reservoir of feeling in matter of being. Removed the self expressed the weight of its existence. So clear the minds sees. So clear the mind frees. But Nini clung to the defense of the people of her moving. And with her cunt opening and closing the consciousness of her life was seen. Now she lost herself. Lost in a river of forced freedom against the power beating in her brain. Beating wildly but

the body ploughed on. To feeling. To discovery. And all that was seen was original fear. Now exposed to the world removed from props and clutches she was dying night and day. Now possessed by feeling and thin lines of shapes called consciousness she felt that she had changed. In depths of feeling and being her world remained the same. The self divided a dichotomy of her age. Grown into nothing but the shelled self of unmoving.

Manu before a crowd of staring eyes screaming his words of penetrating experience more by his antics and language so strange to their ears. At this place of ridiculous pretensions and the sight of beautiful young sisters rushing to fill their minds with the new learning and caught in vice of men who longed to enter that mountain of feeling. All becoming vehicles as smooth flesh so tender and burning with feeling. After all the talk let's get to the women! So beautiful they are and so used. Manu before a crowd of faces the women straining with understanding. Some brothers voicing their appreciation and others in the bar drowning their faces. And Manu so filled with feeling before the faces black and seeing.
If you can understand that you're here because they've taken everything from you. Everything. Why did we move to this place driven by death conquered with death ruled by death all motion is death? Do you love the colour of their faces or the beauty of their heidious lives? Or are we so masochistic we love to die in cold? No feeling governs this place. Nothing but despairing lives LOST of all conquest and the internal turbulence of their disorder. Now they have turned to you. Everyone of fucking you so

duped by lies and all possible perfection of unthinking
so comfortable with the fee-
ble safety of yr education.
Did that spare you in 1964?
Will it spare you now? If
you cannot accept the diff-
iculty and responsiblity
that you should bear, that
you should hold tirelessly
in yr bosoms, of the profoun-
dest meaning of being Black
ina world of white faces.
They are building concentrat-
ion camps in Suffolk in Birmingham. Some of you don't
believe it and I'm not being
symbolical or mythical. The
last myth died with yr experience. Some of you students
feel like unconnected tran-
sients in this city of brick
and cold. Well, the camps are
being built into yr minds and
nothing can save you. Not one
motherfucking thing can save
you, do you understand? Except the total realization of
yrselves as part of the larger
Black community that stretches
from here to Birmingham to
Tiger Bay. I hope you dig on
the ramification of what I'm
saying..

Nini in the audience so confused &
gripped with fear. Manu's white
wife walked into the filled hall
& released the yapping dog now at
Manu's feet barking its delight.
Manu's eyes hit the hall's end &
the smiling eyes of his wife so
large with hate. The meeting
broke up and Manu walked out.

Jabu & Abdullah were laughing
& talking with a beautiful black
girl in a mini-skirt & short afro
& shades standing at their sides.
Osei was talking to a tall old man
& both were nodding their heads.
Alex & his friend Frank were sitting on a leather chair. Frank so
tall & straight in a small voice at
the gathered faces before them.

Manu had left without letting any-
body know the silence of his wife
whose breath followed him through
the door. Nini tall & shaken by
the hearing of her ears walked out
into the hall of voices & faces &
drinks. Frank saw the tall sullen
face & stood before her. Smiling
& his face lit like fire with his
bag slung over his shoulder.

Frank
Hello.

Nini
Hello.

Frank
Forgive me for being so bold
but I could not help but talk.
Forgive me. You looked so
lost. It reminded me of my
days back home when someone
saw a ghost. You know, the
Jamaicans say duppy.

Nini
I'm sorry. Do I really look
so bad? I didn't know.

Frank
Forgive me for saying this,
but you look so good.

Nini
Oh no, you must be joking
then.

Frank
You know joke & serious so
close it beyond separation.
Forgive me. Have you met my
friend? This is Alex.

Nini
Oh, we've met before, haven't
we?

Alex
Right. That's right. Did you
enjoy the evening?

Nini
Well, I was so confused. The

man rembled so much & I didn't
know what to think.

Alex
Well, what do you think now?

Nini
Well, I don't know really. It
was so difficult.

Alex
What was so difficult?

Nini
Well, it's hard to say.
Really, I...

Frank
I think the young lady meant
that she was so shaken by
Manu's strength of conviction
that it sort of upset her.

Nini
Yes. That's right. That's it.
He was so convinced. So emot-
ional.

Alex
Well, that's the Black man's
way. To possess everything by
feeling. See the white man
analyses & learns. But we feel.
Like Frank felt that you were
lost & confused.

Frank
Excuse me a minute. I have to
go & piss.

Nini
(laughing) Of course. Look. I
have to go now because my baby
is not too well.

Alex
You have a baby?

Nini
Yes. Didn't anyone tell you?
Three years old. I would love
to continue our conversation.
Do you have a pen? You could
call me at this number. I'm

sorry but I must rush.

Jabu's head turned in their direction
& he nudged Abdullah. Jabu's eyes
went cold & dead & only his superb
hysterical laughter possessed the
life of a record that saved him. The
beautiful girl was now talking to
Abdullah whose hands were behind
his back. Nini walked through the
door & Frank appeared Osei & his
friend were still nodding & the hall
was filled with noise.

B. GUNN, *continued from pg. 56*

Hector: Do you think that
every filmmaker should make
the personal film?

Bill: Yes. That's very important to me. I think even
our leaders had very strong
charismas. Look at Malcolm X,
Martin Luther King. They interested me much before I
knew what they were talking
about or what they were doing.
It was what they were, you see.
Malcolm could have come back
from Africa a Christian and I
think he would have been listened
to as to why, because of him, BE-
CAUSE OF HIM. But we have a lot
of black artists-who I don't att-
ack-in their plays are chopping
off black peoples heads. The next
thing they end up in uniforms
telling you what to do. You see,
cause that's what it was all about
in the first place. I was very
fortunate to come up at the right
time, the right age, at the right
point. Someone said the 70's are
an incredible time, the 60's was
the revolution, pride and everything else; the 70's are the time
of total reality-about what,who
you are.

continued on pg. 61

OK, so the big question is how do I get sufficient protein? The answer is by eating vegetable protein, beans, nuts, nutitional protein boosters such as wheat germ, brewer's yeast, also whole grain breads and cereals.

One more fact about meat and meat-eaters, meat as a high-protein stimulate food acts upon the mind in a particular way, it tends to bring upon an aggressive, violent nature. An example that comes to mind is the following quotation "A man of war & violence does not eat grain before battle. War demands meat and swords require blood." So remember meat is an expensive second-hand food material and will not make healthy pure blood or form good tissues.

Another poison invading our communities is alcohol. It comes in many forms and strengths and all have a detrimental effect on the body and mind. Alcoholics suffer from the same problems as drug addicts they must have a drink or they go through mental or physical changes.

And what does all this alcohol (wine, beer, scotch, brandy, rum, gin and vodka on and on) do for the human body. It destroys Vitamins C and B, also many valuable minerals, especially magnesium. It is associated with or is known to be a cause of the following diseases: high blood pressure, cirrhosis of the liver, stomach ulcer, asthma, diabetes, gout, neuritis, strokes and heart disease.

Alcohol is very high in calories (196 calories per ounce) once it is consumed by the body it readily changes into fat, causing the amount of blood fat to double which in turn slows the blood flow which is the source of many of the above diseases.

Alcohol supplies no nutrients therefore it is of no food value. It offers the body nothing to build with but turns around and destroys vitality. It calls for enormous amounts of the B complex vitamins and magnesium to be replaced because they are destroyed by alcohol.

Alcohol also has a direct effect on the functioning of the brain. It widens the cerebral ventricles in the brain which leads to dementia. Dementia is defined as "Loss of mental coordination to such a degree that one is insane." I'm sure we've all witnessed this on the streets, that staggering, drunken stupor-dangerous?

It's been also demonstrated that very heavy alcohol consumption decreases brain protein synthesis, whtch means the brain cells cannot utilize the protein necessary to build new cells. This protein being rich in the B Vitamin complex is wasted and the need for B vitamins is increased, and brain damage results. Alcoholics should eat foods highly rich in protein & vitamins to offset some of its lack of these important nutients.

Remember alcohol is a poison as does inhibit normal functioning of the brain, the nerves, the heart, the blood, the liver and the kidney. It does the body absolutely no good whatsoever. It must be eliminated from the body to ensure a healthy life.

The last poisonous food with no nutritional value I wish to deal with is sugar. White sugar refined by a chemical process that destroys all the vitamins and minerals is a most harmful food product found in most over the counter foods: candies, cookies and sodas. There have been articles written stating that sugar itself is a drug. One basis for this argument is that in the refining process everything that has any food value (vitamins & minerals) has been removed thus leaving a pure carbohydrate form. Pure carbohydrates do not exist in nature, so white sugar becomes as harmful as a drug, since our bodies are geared for pure natural food products. Since sugar is such an unnatural product the body relates to it as a stimulant food, and it has the same addicting qualities as drugs.

I have known a woman who has to have her Pepsi everyday before she gets out of the bed. Once she gets it, she is alright again. Well, I'm sure we have all seen and heard of the craving for sweets found in heroin users and quite often when the user cleans up, he/she will be using three to four times the amount of sugar. Once it is in the blood stream the body begins to crave the sugar more and more. This is due in fact to the low blood sugar level found in the majority of sugar eaters. Sugar also leads to many insulin related diseases such as diabetes, hypoglycemia, not to mention tooth-decay and mental problems.

One basic rule must be adhered to in the choice of foods that are to be eaten. All food must have some nutritional and body building value, if it does not it is dangerous and an obstruction to normal body functioning. Once we realize which foods are good and which are bad we must eliminate those which do not enhance the natural body. Also we must get into the practice of body cleansing and purifying, which I will deal with in my next article extensively.

Blessings

Any inquiries concerning my articles and information pertaining to them can be made through Impressions Magazine.

B. GUNN, *continued from pg. 59*

Hector: Because of your position you have become a type of black spokesman, so that I think the images that you deal with have to be perhaps in some way instructive in terms of the total problem... to help see it clearer.

Bill: The only thing that I am compelled to do is make my images true to my imagination. That's all. I mean, if they sit there in the theater and really see, that's all I ask. The black audiences has to learn how to see it's artists, to listen to it's artists Don't turn your artists into politicians.

Hector: ...and how does that happen? Doesn't that happen during the process of what you do with your art?

Bill: Fine, the artists should really be the leaders. In the best societies they have been. We're in a period where we're really sick of politicians, it just happened a few minutes ago. People don't know what's good. I think a personal film can be a very political film. A personal film doesn't have to be someone out in a field picking daisies. It can be a very political film. I think The Battle of Algiers was a very personal film... a very personal film. Ganja & Hess had a lot of detached ideas before I got it into my head that the main thing is that I had given them a different kind of human being. He was silent, but he was different and that was the impact. Then because of him they listened. Imagine if I would have come out and said Bang-this was the message and Bang-another message. But the character made it happen despite all these messages coming at you. You've got to rub their belly until they calm down and forget themselves (audience) TOTALLY for that hour & a half while they're at the theater..totally forget themselves.

Hector: Is that what you want to do with your film?

Bill: Yes, it's what happens. Why, when we're having a depression and starvation...why is there a movie industry boom. Because people aren't in there thinking about their rats & roaches and their food stamps. Maybe they're watching Barbara Streisand chase a trolley down the street but that's interesting. Escape is what they go to that movie for. They don't want you telling them about their rats and roaches because they know what that's about. All that inflated politics that you see on the screen is not real. If you try to apply it to your life, it doesn't fit. It destroys a lot of people and a lot of people who try freak out. Filmmaking is an art, it is the new painting. Paintings have to move now, they just can't hang on the wall and look at you. They can't do that anymore. They have to move now. It has to come out at us and say something. Filmmakers are the Rembrants and the Van Gogh's of this generation. Paintings are now either coming out of the canvas or moving around the wall. They're desperately trying to become films.

Hector: Black filmmakers don't seem to be moving in that direction...?

Bill: No. That's because we got all this political business. I mean, I'm sure I'm more political then anyone else making films out there, that's how it ends up. But that's not how I get the film idea. I got the idea through my senses, to me its a very sensuous act. The problem is that the audience takes the wrong people too seriously. Just because a person's black and he he runs film through a camera that doesn't mean that you have to deal with him seriously. If our kids aren't going to see Black junk, they're going to see white junk. The hardest thing is to get them to see a good film. I've seen young black kids sitting in a very good film and not enjoying it. I've seen an audience of black kids sitting, seeing the Battle of Algiers and they got off on all the wrong things.

Hector: Why do you think black people are so drawn to film?

Bill: I think that the blackman and woman — that we are the truly contemporary people, the expert. You travel through Europe, everyone is emulating the Americans, everyone wants to be American. What is the most interesting thing about Americans? What is it that has made America different than any other country? Why hasn't America become Canada or Australia-it's black people. We are the truly 20th century people and the visual art of film is the 20th century idea. Well, we have been kept off from this, this is why we're in front of the damned T.V. set all the time, just watching images, images, images. We're not 17th,18th century people. All those centuries we were getting our ass kicked in slavery. I'm talking about the American Black not the African. We have come to life in this century, into our own. So we look at what we can see, we deal with it and try to make a difference in what we have and it's not connected with what we see- it's connected with the meaning itself, the idea itself-the eye. The film the medium of film is what attracts us. I think finally when our Black filmmakers get the power and I think this generation is where our filmmakers are starting to come from. ✿

Happenin's

THEATER

THE FIRST BREEZE OF SUMMER
Negro Ensemble Company
St. Mark's Playhouse
133 Second Ave.
674-3530

THE WIZ
Majestic Theater
245 W. 44th St.
246-0730

THE PAST IS THE PAST
WRITTEN BY RICHARD WESTLEY
MANHATTAN THEATER CLUB
321 E. 73rd ST.
BU8-2500
APRIL 24-MAY 11th

RAISIN
46TH STREET THEATER
WEST OF B'WAY
541-6350

SIZWE BANZI IS DEAD / THE ISLAND
EDISON THEATER
240 W. 47th ST.
757-7164

POETRY/ART
TASTE OF ENDLESS FRUIT
LOVE POEMS AND DRAWINGS
BY LEROY CLARKE
840 MONTGOMERY ST.
BKLYN,N.Y. 11213

BLACK PHOTOGRAPHERS ANNUAL
55 HICKS STREET
BKLYN, N.Y. 11201

THE 1199 GALLERY AT 310 W. 43rd ST.
IS NOW SHOWING THE PAINTINGS AND
SCULPTURE OF CAROLE BYARD AND VALEI
MAYNARD, THROUGH JUNE 5, 1975

ALVIN AILEY
CITY CENTER
55th ST. THEATER
APRIL 15-MAY 4

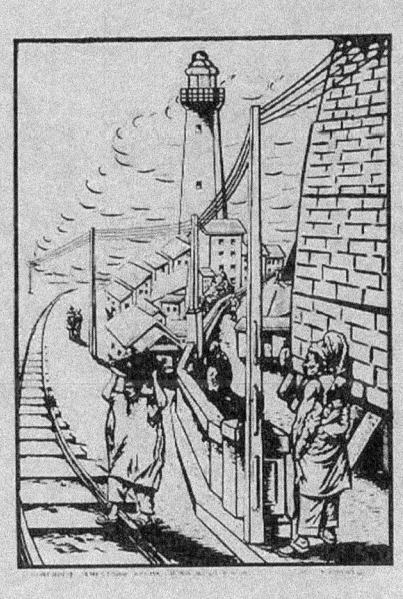
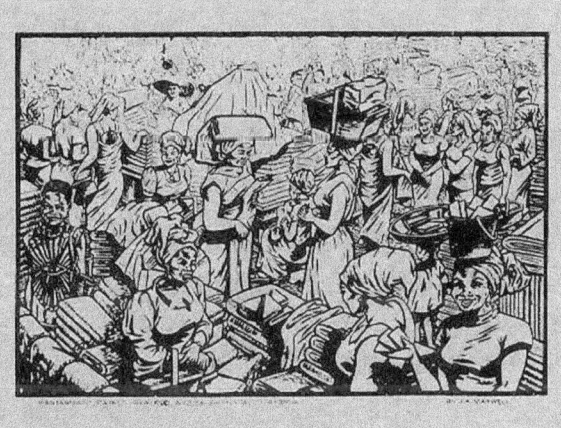

PUBLISHER ACKNOWLEDGEMENTS

The rebirth of the Special 1974 Commemorative Reissue Series of IMPRESSIONS Magazine of the Arts
is a special labor of Love for us. 1974 witnessed an explosion of powerful & creative expressions in:
Theater Arts, Poetry, Art, Music, Photography, Literature, Dance / Choreography,
Theater Review, Film, Critique, Nutritional Advice & Fashion.

As the independent Publisher of IMPRESSIONS MAGAZINE OF THE ARTS I am very proud to be able to again
re-introduce to this new generation, the power and fertile imagination of these generous and talented contributing
artists and creators, who worked so hard to honestly represent themselves and their people
during this tumultuous, passionate and exciting period.
IMPRESSIONS MAGAZINE is truly a historical and educational snapshot of the times.

FERN STANFORD	BILL GUNN
THEODORE STANFORD	HERB HENRY
RICHARD WESLEY	BARON JAMES ASHANTI
BOB WISDOM	MICHAEL BARNES
HECTOR LINO, JR.	BOB ELLISON
ASKIA MUHAMMAD TOURE	RENNIE GEORGE
CALVIN WILSON	BILL WILSON
NIKKI COLEMAN	RONALD K. GRAY
BRENDA BAILEY	LONNIE LISTON SMITH
EUGENE REDMOND	ROBERT BRYAN
RHONDA MILLS	SEBASTIAN CLARKE
IBN MUKHTARR MUSTAPHA	DINDGA MCCANON
OSSIE ONUORA ENEKWE	CLIFFORD GLOVER
FRANK JOHN	CLEVELAND KEELER
ZIZWE OMOWALE WA NAAFUA	

GV SERIES IMPRESSIONS Magazine of the Arts Publications

GV16 **IMPRESSIONS Magazine of the Arts (December 1974)** -Reissue Date 07/29/2012
GV17 **IMPRESSIONS Magazine of the Arts (Spring 1975)**   - Reissue Date 08/15/2012
GV18 **IMPRESSIONS Magazine of the Arts (October 1975)**   - Reissue Date 11/2012
GV19 **IMPRESSIONS Magazine of the Arts (June 1976)**   - Reissue Date 12/2012

With much love & respect, I sincerely thank you from the top of my heart.

Robert Bob Bryan, Founder / Publisher
Loida Bryan, Co-Executive Producer
website: http://www.graffitiverite.com
e-mail: bryworld@aol.com

www.ingramcontent.com/pod-product-compliance
Lightning Source LLC
Chambersburg PA
CBHW081241180526
45171CB00005B/505

9 781479 119844